RAINCOAST CHRONICLES
14

Fish Hooks & Caulk Boots

by

Florence Tickner

with a foreword by Howard White

HARBOUR PUBLISHING

In memory of Mother

RAINCOAST CHRONICLES 14
Fish Hooks & Caulk Boots
Copyright © 1992 by Florence Tickner

HARBOUR PUBLISHING
P.O. Box 219
Madeira Park, BC Canada V0N 2H0

Edited by Perry Millar
Cover painting by Jim Spilsbury
Printed and bound in Canada

The assistance of the Canada Council and the Cultural Services Branch, Ministry of Municipal Affairs, Recreation and Culture, Government of British Columbia are gratefully acknowledged.

Photographs:
All photographs are from the private collection of the author's family, with the exception of the following: pp. 18, 19, 60, 61, private collection, John Macdonald; pp. 22, 51, 77, 78, private collection, Avis Unwin; p. 23, Vancouver Maritime Museum; pp. 25, 74, Campbell River & District Museum; pp. 26, 27, 31, *Raincoast Chronicles*; pp. 47, 71, 75, private collection, Bernice Lawson

Canadian Cataloguing in Publication Data

Tickner, Florence, 1930–
    Raincoast chronicles 14: fish hooks & caulk boots

(Raincoast chronicles, ISSN 0315-2804 ; 14)
    ISBN 1-55017-078-3

    1. Tickner, Florence.   2. British Columbia —
Biography.   I. Title.   II. Series.
FC3825.1.T53A3 1992   971.1'3103'092
F1088.T53A3 1992   C92-091610-4

Contents

Foreword

NORTH OF THE RAPIDS, BC's mainland coast dissolves into a splatter of islands and inlets that old towboaters used to refer to as "the jungles," not because the coastal rainforest grew thicker there than elsewhere, but because the area presented such a tangled profusion of small independent "gyppo" logging operations. Most densely concentrated around the area between Knight and Kingcome inlets, this was the centre of the float camp universe, complete with floating villages at Simoom Sound, Clayton Bay and Sullivan Bay. Their capital was the semi-floating metropolis of Minstrel Island. It was here that Martin Allerdale Grainger set his classic 1908 novel *Woodsmen of the West* and it was here that the social culture of the gyppo logger recorded its most extreme evolutionary progress. It is an area that has always held a special fascination for *Raincoast Chronicles*.

Few are better qualified to describe day-to-day life in that unique universe than the author of this issue, Florence Tickner. Mrs. Tickner spent her childhood riding her father's floatcamp from island to cove to inlet during the thirties and forties, the third generation of her family to experience the singular charms of life in the mid-coast jungle.

We have printed stories from the Minstrel Island area before, most notably in issue twelve, but they tended to bear the stamp of semi-degenerate old bush apes who did not much resemble Mrs. Tickner's picture of the logger as a courtly soul who never cussed. Jim Mackay, for one, cussed so conspicuously I am surprised she couldn't hear him up at Port Elizabeth cussing down at Minstrel, thirty miles away.

No matter. The particular value of Mrs. Tickner's memories of coastal life is that she presents it for once from the viewpoint of the women and children who were the heart and soul of the gyppo world, enlarging on her own experiences with those of of her aunts, her mother, her grandmother and all the camp women in their seagoing network. It has been one of our frustrations over the years that so few pioneer accounts of have been forthcoming from coastal women, and this influenced our decision to break with past practice and devote this entire issue to the work of one author, Florence Tickner. We hope you find her story of domestic life among the floatcamps as refreshing as we do.

HOWARD WHITE

Preface

This is my mother Mabel Kimball, holding me, with Barbara, Ted and Shirley standing below.

LOGGING WAS A WAY OF LIFE for my family. My father was Ed Kimball and his stepfather was Charlie Moore. The Moores had logged near Bellingham, Washington for several years before moving to British Columbia. Dad was five years old when he, his mother, sister Ada, brother Everett, stepfather Charlie and other family members travelled up the coast on the steamer *Comox* to work for the Emerson Logging Company. For the first year or two the family logged in Jervis Inlet, then moved to Drury Inlet. Around 1908 the camp moved to Actaeon Sound, and still later back to Drury Inlet again.

My mother, Mabel McGarvey, had grown up partly in the city, although her family had ties to logging also. Her grandpa Steve Anderson had logged and her grandma had cooked in the camps; her aunt Flo had married Earl Broyles, whom Dad later worked for; her brother Gordon (Uncle Bunt) worked in logging too.

In 1925, when my parents married, they lived on a house float tied to shore at the site of the logging show. I was the youngest of four children, Shirley, Barbara and Ted preceding me. We grew up on a float at the logging sites in and around the entrance to Knight Inlet until the family moved to Gibsons in 1941.

The floats were made of cedar logs because cedar floated highest in the water. A smaller log was pulled onto each end and the logs were lashed to it. A float might last twenty or twenty-five years if it was made of good logs; some floats lasted even longer if they were tied up close to fresh water so mussels and barnacles didn't grow on them.

We always maintained that Uncle Earl Broyles logged at the head of the inlet in Thompson Sound

in later years because it was the only place the camp would stay afloat. The floats were almost sinking—some had come from Moore's camp, and dated back to before 1910—but the abundance of fresh water kept the weed and barnacle growth down, and he was tied up in shallow water, with some extra logs pulled under the floats that probably touched bottom at low tide.

A logging camp might consist of from six to twenty floats. The owner would have a house, and perhaps another house or two would be occupied by families. The remaining buildings would be a cookhouse, some bunkhouses, a wash house, a store house, sheds for tools and equipment and maybe a blacksmith shop. Most camps also had a wood float for fuel, a donkey float, a winch float, a drag-saw float and sometimes an oil float. The floats were positioned along the shore in a sheltered bay with a stream for water close by.

The floats holding machinery could be moved easily as they were needed. The others stayed put until it was time to move to a new location. Then they would be towed to the new site, usually by the tug that towed the logs to the mill.

In our camp, some of the house floats had fences around them to keep small children away from the water; most children, like myself, learned to swim before they were six. We had a nice fenced-in area on one side of our house; Mother even had some snow-on-the-mountain and honeysuckle growing in big tubs on the deck. Our house was very small. It consisted of a lean-to bedroom and one large room, which was living room, dining room and kitchen combined. There was also a pantry, used for storing dishes and cooking supplies, with a sink at the end and a window over it. There was no running water for the sink, but it drained into the salt water. When I was around four years old, Dad added a bedroom to the other side of the house, big enough for a double bed and a single bed, plus a small wood heater. This addition also had a closet with

drawers at the bottom. Before this, a small closet and chest of drawers in the lean-to was our only storage space for clothes. This doesn't seem like much room, but most of the clothes we had were either being worn or they were in the wash.

Our cookstove had a warming oven above and a water reservoir on the side. It was kept going all day and provided heat for the whole house, except for the cold winter days when the heater in the bedroom would be lit also. These stoves kept my dad busy at least one Sunday a month, cutting wood. The house was finished on the inside with V-joint and wasn't insulated, so it took plenty of wood to keep it warm. We children, especially my brother Ted and I, helped a lot stacking wood and cutting kindling. That little house, with its lack of space, comfort, style or any modern conveniences, was a loving home to us, and we wished for no other.

Our floathouse home, with the storage shack on the right. Note the fenced-in area.

Elizabeth (Gram) Moore, Margaret Moore, Everett Kimball, Ada Kimball, Mrs. Edwards, Ernie Edwards, an unknown man in cap; Below, Ernie Moore, Ed Kimball (Dad), unknown man in glasses and Earl Broyles.

Dad

MY FATHER HAD ARRIVED UP NORTH before he was five years old. In a very short time he was swimming, rowing, fishing and taking part in everything else he could. In 1910 or 1911 the camp was logging at Huaskin Lake in Drury Inlet, yarding the logs to the top of the ridge, then skidding them into the salt water. The men had built a log slide that worked very well, as the water was nice and deep and the logs didn't hit bottom and get the ends broken up. It wasn't very far from the lake to the salt chuck, and it was a pretty good setup.

Dad used to hike to the lake and fish for trout. Once when he went there, he accidentally knocked some bark and rotting wood into the water, and a nice-size trout came up to take a look-see. On closer examination, Dad saw that there were grubs in the rotting wood, and trout were lying in

wait below. He quickly got to work, found some grubs and caught several beauties.

It was a carefree life for him, and the only thing he really didn't go for was school. However, it was a necessary evil, and with some prodding from his elders he managed quite well. Everett, Dad's older brother, was not a scholar and as soon as possible he left fractions and Shakespeare and took on board feet and caulk boots. By 1912, Everett and Ada, Dad's sister, had taken eight years of correspondence and Dad had endured seven. Then Dad's mother moved to Vancouver with the three children, and they maintained a house there until Dad finished school, going back to the camp only for the summer holidays. Uncle Everett quit school and started working when he was fifteen, but Dad finished just in time to enlist in the army, although he was only sixteen. After basic training, he was put on guard duty on the trains. On December 6, 1917, his train was in Toronto when the great Halifax explosion occurred. Their train was ordered east to help with the rescue operations. Dad never liked to talk about it, and it must have been a terrible experience. Much of the city was destroyed and hundreds of people were killed.

After the war, Dad went up to the Queen Charlottes to work in a logging camp. He was only up there for a short time and hadn't been paid yet when Christmas was imminent. Oh, how he wanted to get home for Christmas! So he scraped a bit of money together, hitched a ride over to Prince Rupert and paid his fare to O'Brien Bay. By that time he was flat broke. Meals on the boat were 50 cents each, so he talked the situation over with the other men on the boat, and they got a little scheme going. At each meal the other men all threw their 50 cents onto the middle of the table and Dad pretended to do the same. The poor Chinese waiter collected the money and realized one person hadn't paid, but never could figure out who it was.

Shortly after returning to the Charlottes to work, Dad contracted the flu. I guess it was a near thing, but he survived and went back home to regain his strength. Dad was still only eighteen years old and after getting his health back was persuaded to take a business accounting course at Sprott–Shaw school in Vancouver. From stories I have heard, he spent a great deal of time playing for a semi-professional baseball team, where he broke his nose, but he did manage to learn enough to keep books for himself and his partners in later years. He went back up north after his stint in Vancouver, and worked with Ed McLean, Moore Brothers and others.

Dad always enjoyed outdoor activities—almost any kind available. At least twice he hiked "over the hump" from Bond Sound to Kingcome Inlet to visit the Hallidays, who had one of the earliest pre-emptions in the area. I don't know how far that is, but it took a long day to do it. I suppose his main reason was to have a visit with the Hallidays—he was kind of sweet on Jean for a while—but he enjoyed doing it too. Also it was a grand opportunity to get in some duck and goose hunting. The sloughs at Kingcome were alive with wildlife, and the hunting was wonderful.

It was a boat day when Dad dislocated his left shoulder. He was walking along a log when some bark slipped off, and Dad went with it. He instinctively reached around to grab the log, and clunk, out went the arm. He let out a holler, and friends came and hauled him out of the water. One of the men grabbed his arm, gave a mighty pull around, and luckily it slipped back into place. He was only off work for a couple of days, because at that time he was running donkey and, although it hurt, he was able to carry on. It was a long time before he was very effective with an axe, though. Dad spent much of his active life "in the woods," but he was a careful man and never hurt himself seriously.

After Mother and Dad were married, Dad worked for Bruce Macdonald, Uncle Ben Willett, who had married Dad's sister Ada, and several others. He had got his ticket for running a steam donkey, so much of the time that was his job, but he did other work too. Running donkey was good in a way. Dad liked it because in bad weather he stayed pretty dry, and also he didn't have to wear caulk boots all the time. But there were drawbacks. Work started at eight in the morning, and by that time the boiler was expected to have a head of steam, so Dad had to rush over and light a fire in the firebox before he had breakfast. He had to get up really early when he was working for Middy Levesque, because the donkey was back in the woods at the cold deck pile. All this for four dollars a day! These were mainly smaller gyppo outfits that my father worked for, so most of the time there wasn't anyone extra for cutting wood. Steam donkeys gobbled it up, so that meant a lot of Sundays on the woodpile.

After the logs were yarded into the water, they had to be boomed up. Most of the time they were divided into three types: cedar, fir and others. Occasionally the cedar was rough graded, and a section of number one logs was kept separate to try to get a better price. Dad liked working on the boom; he was really quick on his feet too. He could go for days without getting his feet wet, and I hardly ever remember him falling in the water.

The Handlogger

THE INDEPENDENT MAN—that was the handlogger. He was a loner, although he enjoyed the odd bit of company. Some of the old-time handloggers probably lived by themselves because they couldn't get along with anyone else on a long-term basis. They were stubborn, generally preferring to do things their own way, even if it took twice as long. They were satisfied just to make a living and were not interested in accumulating a lot of this world's goods. After working for perhaps two or three months to get out a section or more logs, this hardy fellow would sell them, buy some staples to last until the next logs were sold, and then, more than likely, go on a big "toot." The celebration would last until the poor man ran out of money or got good and tired of other people's company.

Handlogging permits were easily obtained. After a suitable place was found, where trees could be cut and easily skidded into the water, the handlogger would mark the location on a map and apply to the Forestry Department. In 1930, a deposit of ten percent of stumpage fees was required, plus two dollars for a marking hammer, or stamping hammer as we called them. The first thing a logger did on getting his hammer was hang it, drill a hole at the butt of the handle and string a thong through—it was very easy to drop the hammer into the water but sometimes pretty hard to get it out.

Then the work would begin. First, a few small trees had to be cut down cross-ways to a selected big tree to give it something to skid on. Then the big tree was cut down across the bed of small trees, and accuracy was very important. Next, the big tree was sniped and barked on one side. The barking was done as fast as possible, because the wetter the tree was the easier it would skid and slide into the water. During and after barking, the Gilchrist jack came into its own. Without this heavy, cumbersome tool, the logger would have been hard pressed to get the logs into the water. The peavey was also a must. It was used along with the jack to turn and rock the trees so they would start to slide. Finally the tree would slip into the water, and then it would have to be tied up. Later the top would probably have to be sawed off, and sometimes the tree would be cut into two or three logs, using a bucking saw, to improve the scale.

Not too many tools were needed for handlogging. A falling saw, and one for bucking, three different axes, a sledgehammer and wedges, the jack and peavey. When the logs were in the water, some other tools were needed: a few eyed spikes called dogs and some strawline or rope to hold the logs together, a pike pole and an auger. The auger was a simple tool but at the same time by far the most gut-wrenching. It was used to drill holes into the ends of specially selected sixty-six-foot logs for use as boomsticks and swifters. These logs were used to surround the other logs and make up a boom, or section. Imagine using a hand tool to make a hole in a good-sized log large enough for a boom chain to fit through! It was back-breaking, and heaven help you if you ran into a knot. It was very important to keep all tools sharp and rust-free. In that climate and working around the salt water, tools rusted and dulled easily.

It's easy to understand why some of these fine, hard-working men occasionally turned to the bottle, or became a little "odd." Some handloggers were very fussy about personal cleanliness, but others got pretty careless over the years. Grey Stanfield underwear was much preferred. It didn't show the dirt nearly as bad as the white or yellowish type. And some shirts and pants got pretty stiff before they were changed. Uncle Ben Willett and a friend were timber cruising one time and stopped in to visit an old handlogger who was working in the area. The man was delighted to see them and asked them to stay for lunch. With some reluctance they accepted, and they walked into his cabin, the old fellow talking all the while. This man always had a pipe clenched between his teeth – lit or unlit – and he just talked around it. Anyway, when the men got to the cabin, the old handlogger proceeded to make a batch of biscuits, talking continuously, pipe in mouth and "dottle" from the pipe dripping now and then into the dough. It must have been fascinating – and at the same time revolting – watching all this, knowing you were going to eat the mixture. It didn't kill them, but they sure never went back there for lunch!

One fellow I remember was Frank Benjamin. He had a little place near the mouth of Bond Sound that

that he needed some company, so he headed to Vancouver, and when he arrived back up north he had a wife in tow. Not long after they got back, Tom Hyde came to their house and knocked. Mrs. Duffy answered the door and asked him in. He just stood there and said, "No thanks, I just came over to see what kind of woman would marry that man Duffy."

Any logger I can remember from when I was a child used tobacco in one way or another. Most men smoked cigarettes which they rolled by hand. These went out when they were put down, so were safer than tailor-made ones – cheaper too. Uncle Ben smoked a pipe or cigars, and I remember Aunt Ada "gently" reminding him to clean his pipe, as it made so much noise when he sucked it. And then there were the snuff users and to-

he had pre-empted in 1912. He was a nice man, always polite and quiet and very shy with women. On boat day he would come putt-putting along in his little open gas boat, pick up his mail, groceries and supplies, chat with my uncle for a few minutes and then head for home again. If he didn't show up, someone would check up on him to make sure everything was all right. He lived there for years, logging just enough to keep him going, and seemed very happy and content.

There was a small island in Thompson Sound that handloggers liked, and over the years many permits were issued for it. While officially logging on the island, the men really spent most of their time poaching trees from the surrounding mainland, which was steep and well suited to this illegal activity. The forest rangers seemed to turn a blind eye to the situation.

Tom Hyde handlogged in Thompson Sound for several years. He had a little shack on a float pulled up to the highest tide mark, so it was almost like living ashore. Jack Duffy also logged in Thompson Sound, but the two men didn't get along, even though at that time they didn't have any close neighbours. Jack Duffy finally decided

bacco chewers. The person with a cheek bulge was easily identified as a tobacco chewer with a "cud." If you saw a bulge of the lower lip you could be sure that person was using snuff. Uncle Everett did, and boy, could he ever spit! Ted and I used to watch him when he was working around camp; he teased us by seeing how close he could come to our feet. It was fun when he was inside too, because we would wait to see how long it took before he had to go outside to spit. (We didn't have a spittoon in the house, though he used the stove sometimes.)

If times were tough, the old-time logger had many ways to make things last. They were "haywire" experts as far as fixing anything was concerned. The caulk boots had to be sharp, and if they were good boots like Paris or Dayton, new caulks could be put in if the old ones got dull. Leckie boots were also available, but unless our hero was really hard up he didn't buy "Leaky Leckies." He had a way with socks too. When the heels wore out he turned the socks over and wore the heels on top. When that wore out, he cut off the toe, roughly sewed up the leg part and wore them backwards!

"Uncle" Owen and Other Old-Timers

EVEN WHEN I WAS A YOUNGSTER in the thirties, there weren't many people living along the coast. We knew a lot of them in the area above Alert Bay and had heard of most of the others. Of course some were special, and they were our "uncles."

"Uncle" Owen Waite was an old man when I knew him, craggy-faced, long and lean, and he still had an Ozark twang to his speech. He boasted that he never went to school a day in his life, but when he was an adult he taught himself to read and write, so he certainly wasn't lacking in brains. There wasn't much reading material in camps in those days, but everything there was, he read: the big catalogues from Woodwards, Eaton's and equipment companies, and the popular pulp magazines.

Owen handlogged, worked with partners and in later years worked for my uncle Earl Broyles. He seldom went to Vancouver, preferring to watch camp while the others went. He was a wonderful man with an axe; chopping wood or even building a donkey sled was right up his alley. In fact, he was a real fix-it man, repairing almost anything that could be repaired. He could build things too. I remember a rowboat he made. It was eight or nine feet long, solid, and didn't leak a drop. He had built it all by hand, sawing the boards, shaping the oars and making the pegs. Yes, he used wooden pegs instead of nails or screws.

Uncle Owen claimed he never got sick, but the time came, when he was in his eighties, that he was feeling poorly and decided to go to Vancouver. He died soon after arriving there, and the autopsy showed a calcification the size of a golf ball on one lung. It had been rubbing on his heart, and the doctor said it must have taken years to grow to that size. He had never seen anything like it. They made them tough in those days!

"Uncle" Jim Shope worked up north for years too. He had come when he was a young man from

somewhere in the southern United States, but never seemed to miss his own country. He worked at handlogging and at different times in partnership with Carl Stamey, Owen Waite and my real uncle, Frank Anderson. Jim wasn't above a bit of bootlegging on the side, either. In later years he worked for Harry Cyr.

Carl Stamey, Aunt Min and Jim Shope.

Uncle Jim was always ready for a couple of drinks and a good poker game, but what we children liked the best was when two or three of the men got together and started to reminisce. They could go on and on about how good—or bad—the logging was at a certain place, or how incompetent the last cook was, or how far away that three-point buck was when they shot it. And we would sit and listen—sometimes getting a sip of home-brew beer—and do you know, we never heard a swear word! "Gosh all hemlocks" or "By damn" was pretty rough stuff.

Carl Stamey was a young, good-looking man and I think he had a crush on Mother before she and Dad were married. Anyway, he named his boat the *Mabel*, and we still have pictures of it.

Uncle Earl Broyles was married to my mother's aunt Flo, but not for very long. They were divorced when I was four or five years old. It was the first time I had heard of anything like that, a real scandal at the time too. Earl had come from Arkansas as a young man and retained a slight southern drawl all his life. He was a real gentleman—a gentle man too—always courteous, and he would never think of using strong language around women.

When he first went up north, Earl handlogged with Billy Yelton, then later worked for Moore Brothers Logging, and still later went into partnership with them. Broyles and Moore carried on until 1935, when the last of the Moores moved to Vancouver and Earl took over the camp by himself. I remember his first boat, the *Fujiyama*, rotting on the beach in Thompson Sound.

There were two Lansdowne families up north. The men were brothers, and one settled at the head of Kingcome Inlet, the other on a farm across from Alert Bay. They were a colourful bunch, or perhaps eccentric would be a better word. Buster and Edgar were two boys from the Alert Bay family, and they were always up to some mischief. Their dad's big bull had chased them a time or two, and they didn't like the animal, so one day they decided to get revenge. They found some dynamite, a cap and fuse, and set it going in the middle of the bull's field. The curious animal came over to investigate the sputtering, and the charge blew up. The bull flew into the air, came down on all four feet and ran. He wasn't seen for two weeks, then returned good as new!

Buster used to stop in to see us occasionally. He usually had a pretty nice boat, as he was in commercial fishing at the time, and we were allowed to look it over. The craft would never win an award for neatness or cleanliness, but the fishing gear was kept in good shape. Buster loved to talk, and as the years went by he talked more, and ever closer to the person he was addressing. Finally, it got to the point where he was talking louder, longer and closer, and the person he was talking to had to keep backing up to avoid getting sprayed!

Guy Lawson went up north in 1906, first to Seymour Inlet, then in 1919 the family moved to Alert Bay. At first, the Moores and Lawsons were logging not too far apart, and young Kathleen, the daughter, got to know Gram Moore very well, calling her Aunt Lizzie. As a young girl, she stayed overnight a few times and still remembers the brass bed—for a long time she thought it was gold! This was during the time the Moores had their camp tied up in McKenzie Sound.

John Dunseith was an early arrival on the coast too. Before 1910 he was also a bookkeeper for Emerson Logging, then married in 1910 and soon after moved with Minnie, his new bride, to Simoom Sound on Gilford Island. They ran a store there for many years, plus the post office. Simoom Sound was an important weekly stop for the Union Steamship Company.

Fritz Salem was another old-timer who drifted around the area between Knight and Kingcome Inlets, with regular appearances in the supply centres of Simoom and Minstrel Island. For a while he had a steamboat called the *Flossie*. At the back of his boat, hidden in the stern, he had a container holding home-brew. A piece of long macaroni was used to suck it up. He was another man with no formal education but seemed to manage just fine. He handlogged for a time in McKenzie Sound on Huaskin Lake.

Things got pretty tough for Fritz and his partner at one point during the Depression, and they heard of work to be had at Prince Rupert, so they decided to give it a try. Their only means of getting around was by rowboat, but that didn't stop them. Some freight for Rupert had been put off at Minstrel by mistake, so they loaded it into the rowboat along with their dog and set off. It took them almost two weeks to get there, and when they arrived they were cold, wet and very hungry. The job rumour turned out to be groundless. The only money Fritz and his pal could raise was five dollars for delivering the freight, so they bought some rolled oats for the dog and a bottle of rum for themselves and headed back to Minstrel. They figured that if they were going to starve, they might as well do it around people they knew. When Fritz finally made a few dollars and bought a gas boat, he called it the *Demerara*!

These are logs coming out of Actaeon Sound. It was quite a sight to watch the logs go endways and sideways in the swift current.

Deadheads

WHEN LOGGING BEGAN on the British Columbia coast, only the biggest and best trees were taken. Fallers even climbed up on springboards to cut the trees down, thus avoiding the swollen butts. They took cedar, fir and spruce and left most of the hemlock; not that hemlock couldn't be used for lumber, but the other types were much better, and they always floated.

The first lumber mill to export its product from British Columbia was built in 1848. This mill was on the upper end of Esquimalt Harbour, Victoria. Before that, tiny mills were built purely for domestic use. In 1849 Captain Walter C. Grant built a small sawmill in Sooke. From this small mill, piles and spars were exported to exotic places like Hong Kong, the Sandwich Islands, Australia and Shanghai. In 1861 a sawmill in Port Alberni, started by Captain Edward Stamp, began produc-

tion. A circular saw imported from England enabled the mill to cut 50,000 board feet in a ten-hour day. In November 1864, after less than four years of operation, the Alberni mill had run out of accessible timber and shut down for good. But Captain Stamp was a stubborn man, and by 1865 he had started another mill, this time in Burrard Inlet. It was called the Hastings Mill and it stood where the city of Vancouver now stands. He paid $240 for Lot No. 196, which is now the heart of Vancouver.

It is interesting to note that Americans began coming to British Columbia around the turn of the century. US President Theodore Roosevelt put 148 million acres of land into national forests during his term in office, and American lumber tycoons felt the pressure. Many moved to BC, including J.H. Bloedel, J.S. Emerson, John J. Stewart and James O. and D.O. Cameron. The

Moore brothers, Henry, Charlie and Ernie, logged in Washington State at Lake Whatcom and Lummi Island before moving to BC in 1904. They worked for J.S. Emerson at first, then started their own camp, selling their logs to Emerson, who had opened a mill at Port Moody in 1905. By 1912 there were 250 sawmills and 350 logging camps working in British Columbia.

The big year for pulp mills in British Columbia was 1909. It saw the start of Port Mellon, Ocean Falls and Powell River, although production didn't start at Powell River until 1912, and in Ocean Falls the first newsprint roll wasn't produced until 1917. The Vancouver *Province* was one of the original customers of the Powell River Company, and in April 1912 produced its first edition from Powell River newsprint. By the fall of 1913, Powell River was running four newsprint machines and turning out 250 tons a day — the fastest in the world at that time.

But while the number of mills and camps was growing, and production was increasing by leaps and bounds, wages and working conditions were not keeping pace. In 1886, $1.25 per day was the going wage at the mills, and skilled workers at the camps were making fifty to sixty dollars per month plus board. When you consider that the days were eleven and a half hours of very hard work — gradually shortened to ten hours as the years went by — it seems pretty small return for the effort. And things weren't much better when the poor man finished work, either. Back he went to the bunkhouse — probably soaking wet — and hung his clothes to dry. Then it was supper time and bed soon after. A straw mattress at best, with rough wool blankets and no sheets, was all he could expect. And his only outlook was another day of the same. You hear people talk of the good old days, but some of them were far from it, I think. Conditions and wages improved slightly until the Depression, when everything slumped badly. Chinese and Japanese workers had their wages cut from forty cents an hour to ten cents. The East Indians received twelve cents per hour

and the white workers got twenty-five cents. Things gradually improved in the 1930s, but it took a strike to do it, and the wages increased to $3.20 per day in 1934.

With the building of pulp mills, the once-lowly hemlock gained new respectability. It was suitable for paper-making, but it had a special drawback: it wasn't very buoyant and many trees sank when they hit the salt chuck. Others floated low in the water, and that meant wet feet booming them up. Many of the low floaters had to be bound to other logs with old cable so they wouldn't drop out of the boom as it was being towed to the pulp mill. Others would stay up only when the men sawed a few feet of the heaviest wood from the butt. All these little extras took time and added to the cost. One hemlock show Dad and his partners were working on was particularly bad for sinkers. What with the trimming and sinkings plus the extra time and work, it was difficult just to break even.

One of the results of this new trade in hemlock was an increase in deadheads — logs which had sunk at one end. They would hang straight down in the water with just an inch or two showing. When anyone was running a boat in that country, they always kept on the lookout for deadheads, because they were so hard to see and they could sink a boat in no time flat.

One time we children were awakened in the middle of the night by a loud thumping under our bedroom floor. It stopped for a few minutes, then thump — thump — thump again. We called Dad and he heard it too, so he went out to investigate. A deadhead had come up between our float logs, and with the movement of the tide, was rising up and hitting the floor of the house. Dad managed to push it down again and direct it away from our float, but it took a bit of doing in that confined space.

Nowadays we see far less waste of marketable logs, mainly because they are bundled before being boomed, while still others are loaded onto big barges. Flat booms made up of single logs are still used, however, and boats still get sunk by deadheads. In the 1950s, I had the awful experience of hitting a deadhead at night in a boat. It was a twenty-eight-foot gillnet-type boat, and she received a gash about six inches wide and three feet long. She sank in about two minutes!

Uncle Ben

Margaret Moore, Bob Lawson and Uncle Ben Willett.

THERE IS USUALLY ONE PERSON in your life whom you remember with fondness and love, whose actions and personality are appreciated by many. Ben Willett was such a person. With his honesty and integrity and his wonderful sense of humour, he was respected and admired by all who knew him. From as early as I can remember, until his death in 1965, no one spoke ill of him, but many spoke with enthusiasm of his good nature, willingness and honesty.

Ben's parents had a farm near New Richmond, on Chaleur Bay, in Quebec. He was born there in 1882, and because he was a good student even went to high school, which was unusual in those days. At that time things were quite depressed back east, but young Ben found work in a grocery store, besides helping on the farm. He had an older brother Harry, who was to eventually take over the farm, so Ben decided to head "out west" to see what work he could find.

In 1905 Ben worked in Vancouver, helping build the foundation of the old Vancouver General Hospital. In 1907 he went into partnership with a married man, handlogging in Drury Inlet. A short time after that he had a small camp of his own, and then he joined up with Moore Brothers. After Ben married my aunt Ada in 1912, he started working for the Provincial Forest Service and stayed with them for about five years. For part of that time he was "loaned" to the Aeronautic Supply Department, issuing spruce permits and licences during World War I.

In 1917 N.C. Jamison offered him a job running camp for the Northern Cedar Logging Company. This was a fairly large outfit based in Everett, Washington, with a camp in British Columbia. Uncle Ben ran the camp in BC for almost six years, and the directors were very sorry to see him go. He had made a financial success of it after several superintendents had failed to do so.

In the thirties, my mother was ill for some time, and I was very lucky to be taken care of by Aunt Ada and Uncle Ben. No doubt they spoiled me rotten, but I loved it. One little episode that I remember is a good example of how soft-hearted Uncle Ben was. I had just awakened from my nap one afternoon and saw Uncle Ben busy on the water, towing a couple of boomsticks. He was real close to the floats so I yelled, "Come and get me!" He said, "I'm too busy right now, Babe!" Then I demanded, "Come and get me just the same!" He did.

Uncle Ben had a wonderful sense of humour. He would laugh and laugh at any funny story or joke that anyone told, but the best part was listening to him tell a joke. Just before he got to the end he would start to laugh, and pretty soon everyone was laughing, and we hadn't even heard the punch line!

We went to movies together in Vancouver in the early days too. If it was a comedy, Uncle Ben would laugh so hard that Aunt Ada would get embarrassed. And in those days there were lots of comedies—Abbott and Costello, Laurel and Hardy, the Three Stooges, Charlie Chaplin—and he loved them all. We almost had to leave the theatre one night. The movie was about logging, and the fallers in this story were like Mutt and Jeff. There they were, sawing down this big tree by hand, and the little fellow was doing all the work. The tree was so big that Shorty couldn't see how little effort his partner was putting forth, and naturally Uncle Ben thought it was hilarious. He just roared, the tears were streaming down his face, and Aunt Ada pretended she didn't know him. If the movie happened to be a love story, a musical or a mystery, in two minutes Uncle Ben was asleep, and he would stay that way until the show was over.

In the early thirties, log prices were very poor, and sometimes it was impossible to sell, unless the timber was number one. Many outfits had

their logs all boomed up, just sitting in the salt water waiting for a buyer, and there they remained. Once a log is dumped into the salt chuck it is prey to "bugs" or teredos, wood-boring mollusks that honeycomb the wood with holes and render it worthless after a few months. Many gyppos were ruined by bugs during this period. Ben managed to hold on until things got better. By 1942, when his camp was sold, prices were on the rise and the outlook for the logging industry was rosy. World War II could take the credit. Uncle Ben left the north with just enough to retire on, but the good feelings he left behind were his real wealth.

In later years Ben went fire spotting up to the Queen Charlottes. Later, with a partner, he owned a pool room, but his heart was always turned toward logging and loggers. I can see him yet, at the wheel of his camp boat the *Rena*, a "Rain Test" canvas hat jammed on his head, his pipe gripped between his teeth and a big grin on his face.

Uncle Ben and Aunt Ada's house in Bond Sound.

Time and Tide

Tide played a very important part in the lives of everyone living upcoast. If they were travelling, it paid them to look at the tide tables to see when the best time was to leave. It was far better to go with the tide than struggle against it. Tugboat captains always watched the tides when they were towing booms. They could get pulled backwards and get into real trouble in places where the tide ran fast.

Any time we had a boom of logs ready for the tug, we hoped the *Prosperative*, with Cal Goodwin as skipper, or the *Prospective* would come to tow them away. We also hoped they would show up and then have to wait a few hours for a suitable tide. During the wait there would be time for a visit and perhaps a game of solo or poker. We children were allowed on the tug for a good look around—Doug Cliff was one skipper who was always good to us—and the cook usually gave us something special to eat. The arrival of the tugs broke the monotony for everyone, and it was always sad to see the boom disappear. Then came the wait, two weeks to two months or more, to find out how the logs scaled out. In those days before cubic metres, wood volumes were measured or scaled in a unit known as the board foot, which was a theoretical piece of one-by-twelve lumber one foot long. Guessing how many of these little square bits were contained in a boom the size of a football field was an inexact science to say the least. The scale also took into account the grade of each individual log, which had a profound effect on the money the logger received, and this added to the suspense.

As youngsters we quickly became aware of tides, and learned to respect their power. We used to row miles from home, with the knowledge that when the tide changed, it was an easy row back. Naturally at times we got caught and had to row for all we were worth to get anywhere against it. We learned at a very early age that often you could get relief from the flow in a bay, where you might even get in a back-eddy and have easy rowing for a while. We enjoyed the challenge of the tide too. I can remember going fishing in the rowboat to White Beach Pass, close to the entrance of Knight Inlet, knowing that when the tide changed it would be a very hard row home. But that didn't daunt us. If we didn't catch anything while the tide was coming in, we would usually fish over high slack, knowing we would be bucking it all the way home. Once, when the tides were extreme, we had to use a pole as well as oars to make any progress against it. We were really lucky not to break an oar on some of our excursions; it would have meant a long wait for the tide to change, as we couldn't paddle against it with any success.

Anyone living on the water soon learned to read the tide tables and knew within a very few minutes what the tides were doing each day. If, in our roamings of the area, we found a good log on the beach, we would try to beachcomb it at high tide. Every now and then we were able to get a log on our own, and naturally we were very proud of our efforts.

Low tide was very important too. If we were going clam digging, we wanted to be there before low slack so the incoming water wouldn't fill up the holes too soon. Then too, fishing always seemed better at low slack, or at least with the tide coming in.

The Halliday home as it still stands in Kingcome Inlet.

We also learned to tie up boats well. If we went ashore in the rowboat, we made sure that we had a long rope and tied it high up on the beach. It's no fun wading out to get a boat in wintertime after the tide has come in faster than you thought it would.

When we were tied up at North Pass, Reg Halliday occasionally stopped in. At that time Reg was running the farm at Kingcome Inlet, and he had developed a market at Alert Bay for his beef, milk products and vegetables. When waiting for an hour or two would give him a favourable tide, Reg sometimes came for a short visit. Dad and Reg had been good friends since childhood, and we always enjoyed his visits. Once he even stayed overnight because of the weather, but that was uncommon, for the *Marybea* was a good sea boat.

Mary, Reg and Lil's youngest child, was about my age, so when I was asked to spend a week at Kingcome, I jumped at the chance. After the first night, when I was terribly homesick, Mary and I had a wonderful time. We played on the swings, fed the horses, helped with the cows and watched butter being made. The milk separator was a real eye-opener for me too, and it was fun being allowed to turn the handle. The day before Reg was due to go on his next trip to Alert Bay and I to go home, a steer was butchered, and I was allowed to help in the skinning. It wasn't as easy

as doing a deer, but by the end of the day it was something I knew a little about.

Mr. and Mrs. Halliday, Reg's parents, were still living then, and although they were getting on in years, they were both able to contribute a great deal to the running of the farm. Mr. Halliday (Gaff) used to preside at the head of the table, and before the evening meal began he said grace. During the meal, if anyone wanted bread, he cut a slice, speared it with the knife and passed it that way. I was very impressed.

It was a rare camp that had more than one power boat when I was a child, but usually there were two or three rowboats or skiffs, and they were used often. Our transportation was at the front door, either tied up or pulled up on a float. It was just as handy as the car in the garage is these days. I suppose the rowing could be equated to walking, and travelling in a power boat could be compared to riding in a car. But it sure was a lot slower. Any boat that travelled over six miles an hour was really speedy in those days.

Uncle Bunt, Mom's brother, and his family were living in Beaver Cove in the thirties—poor, kind of ragged, but getting by. He didn't own a gas boat, only a rowboat, and went to work with the other men in the camp boat. One day the children were all playing outside; my cousin Beverley was in a rowboat which was partly pulled up on a float, and the others were off doing something else. Suddenly, when Bev moved to the back of the boat, it slipped into the water. There was Beverley, all alone, drifting farther and farther from the float. Finally one of the other children spotted her and ran into the house to tell Aunt Lottie. Bev was about three years old at this time, too young to realize the possible consequences of her predicament. The tide was ebbing, and it would take only a few minutes for the boat to drift out into Johnstone Strait. Aunt Lottie was calm on the outside but near to hysteria inside as she gently called to Beverley to put the oars into the oarlocks and get the blades into the water. Bev was too little to row, but she could use one oar at a time while standing up and looking forward in the boat. Slowly but surely the rowboat came back to the float as she pushed on one oar and then the other. It was a happy group that finally grabbed the boat and got Beverley back on the float.

Gaff and Grandma Halliday in the early 1930s.

Oh, Florence, How Could You?

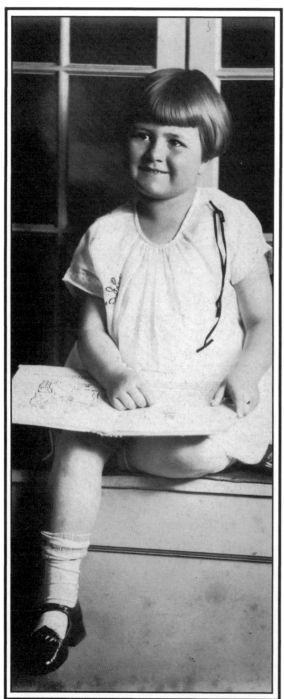

L IFE ON FLOAT HOUSES had many advantages as well as disadvantages. Garbage disposal was a snap—just throw it in the chuck. Certainly no septic tanks or holding tanks were necessary, as the "outhouse" had a direct link to the ocean. Mind you, the two-seater was pretty chilly at times, and it could be wet and dark getting there. Being the youngest child, I could usually talk one of my sisters into going out with me if it was dark when nature called, but I made sure I went last thing before bed, because they wouldn't get up in the middle of the night for me. Of course, we had a chamber pot under the bed too.

At the time, being a child, life was wonderful. When I look back I know there were real hardships, but I never noticed them at the time. We didn't have to pay for water and most of the time we had a good supply, although we packed it into the house because there was only an outside tap or the rain barrel. Mom had to heat water on the stove for any cooking or washing she wanted to do. We didn't have a washing machine either, so the old scrub board was well used. Small clothes were wrung out by hand, but heavier things were put through a wringer. Sometimes one of us children got to turn the handle. I remember when I was pretty little, my brother Ted and I had fun at Moore's camp. Gram Moore was washing blankets in a big tub, and we were allowed to trample in the tub in our bare feet, cleaning the blankets at the same time.

There weren't any taxes to pay on the house either. That was a good thing, as I doubt my parents could have afforded them. One thing they always kept up, though, was fire insurance. You might think that living on the water would keep us safe from fire, but not so. Wood logs were towed to the camp, cut into blocks and hauled onto the float. The green wood produced a lot of creosote, which lodged in the metal chimney pipes, and this created a risk of chimney fires. I remember one chimney fire we had, at night naturally, which burned for almost a half hour. The chimney was red almost to the roof. Creosote burns very hot once it gets started. Yukon flues, which insulated the hot pipes as they passed through the roof, were mandatory in order to get fire insurance, and there were some safety regulations, mostly common sense, that had to be followed. Dad used to clean the chimneys pretty often; that was another one of those "Sunday jobs."

Mother often mentioned the winter when they had fifty dollars to last them through until spring, when the camps would open up again and Dad could earn some wages. I guess we didn't get any new clothes that year, but there was always plenty to eat. In the winter, if Dad had shotgun shells, we ate ducks once or twice a week, with the odd goose as well. Of course, deer was a staple, and there were cod and clams and even the occasional winter spring salmon. Mom did a lot of canning, and we always had canned salmon and deer meat on hand. Canned deer meat stew is still a great favourite of mine.

We never wasted anything, either, and we always had to be careful not to drop things overboard. One time my sister Shirley dropped a flashlight overboard when it was turned on, and we could see it shining down on the bottom for a long time. Usually, if one was retrieved, it was ruined by the salt water anyway.

I still remember how bad I felt when I accidentally threw a pot away into deep water, when I was only supposed to throw out the contents. Mom just said, "Oh, Florence, how could you!" and didn't spank me or punish me, because she knew it was an accident. That made me feel worse than ever.

Every once in a while a boom chain was lost overboard. That was a real disaster, because they were worth around ten dollars.

I wouldn't want to mention any names, but there was a true story told of one unfortunate logger who lost his false teeth overboard. He had gone down to Vancouver to get the teeth and returned as happy as can be. When he got to Echo Bay he started to celebrate, and by the time the boat left he was in pretty bad shape. It was stormy, with rough seas, going back to the camp, and the poor logger got seasick, losing his beer, teeth and everything else over the side!

A long, slow tow to the next camp.

Ted, Shirley, myself and Barb at Uncle Ben's camp in Bond Sound.

The Broken Foot

WHEN WE WERE CHILDREN and on our way ashore to do some exploring, Mother always said, "Watch out for rolling logs." And with good reason. They can cause some pretty bad accidents, even to the point of killing a person.

Mom and Dad were married in August 1925, and by January 1926, birth control being almost unheard of, they were expecting their first child. One afternoon they were duck hunting in Greenway Sound and decided to go ashore on Broughton Island to look around the driftwood. Mother jumped on a log, which started to roll. She lost her balance and fell. The log rolled onto her foot, jamming it against the rocks. She hollered and Dad came running. He tried to move the log, but it was too heavy, and it was going to keep rolling as soon as Mom's foot was out of the way. So he found a long pole and pried the log up, using all his strength. Mother's foot came free and she crawled to safety past the log. Then Dad had to carefully let the pole down and run like anything to get out of the way. Then he ran to Mother, who was in dreadful pain. By this time dusk was falling and a storm was brewing. Dad carried Mother back to the rowboat and rowed back to camp as fast as he could. There she was transferred to a small gas boat and they headed to O'Brien Bay, where they knew a man who had a larger and faster boat. With no hesitation the man said he would take them to the nearest hospital, at Alert Bay, so they set out at once. By then it was black dark and quite stormy.

From O'Brien Bay to Alert Bay is about thirty nautical miles, much of it in the open waters of Queen Charlotte Strait. Imagine, if you can, a small gas boat—no more than twenty-five feet in length—in the winter, in a storm, at night, going perhaps five or six miles an hour. It must have been a terrible trip, every jar of the boat bringing, if possible, more pain to Mother's mashed foot. The journey took nearly six hours, but they made it.

When they finally arrived at the dock and took Mom to the hospital, the doctor looked at the foot, poked at it, wiggled it, asked a couple of questions and then said, "I'll see it in the morning." The next day the doctor looked at the foot again and said, "There is nothing I can do. Keep it up and rest it." So back home they went, with nothing resolved. Mother was still in terrible agony, the foot looked like a blue balloon, and she stayed in pain day and night for months to come. As she got heavier with her pregnancy, the foot swelled more and hurt her constantly.

Finally, in June, the time came to go to Vancouver. As soon as possible after arriving in the "big city," Mother saw a doctor about her foot, but by this time the bones had set and the doctor felt it was best to leave it alone. Mom had pain and swelling in her foot, especially in hot weather, all her life. It was always difficult finding shoes to fit too.

So remember, when your children are going to explore along the driftwood, say to them, "Watch out for rolling logs!"

Alert Bay in the 1920s.

The Union Steamship Company

THE UNION STEAMSHIP COMPANY was formed in 1889 and served the British Columbia coast well and faithfully for seventy years, until its end in 1959. It was the only link to civilization for those who lived "up north." The ships brought news of deaths, wars and disasters, often many days after the fact. Through the mails, the loggers and fishermen could try to keep up with the news from Vancouver, whether it was the latest world crisis or the latest fashion.

The *Comox* was the first vessel that took passengers and freight to isolated spots on the coast, and she was the one that carried my father's family to Jervis Inlet in 1904. She was only 104 feet long, but was licensed for two hundred passengers, and had forty berths after she was rebuilt in 1897. She was pretty speedy for those days too—twelve knots. In 1901 the *Cassiar* was added to the logging camp run. The superstructure of this vessel was built in Vancouver, using the hull of the *J.R. McDonald*, which had been burned. Heading upcoast, these small steamers carried freight, passengers and mail. On the way back to Vancouver—if the season was right—they would have a full load of canned salmon. The time of arrival at the different ports of call varied a great deal, but considering tides, weather and many other problems, they were very faithful.

The *Camosun*, a larger steel-hulled vessel, arrived new from Scotland in 1904. She could carry three hundred tons, whereas the *Comox* was only capable of one hundred. This larger vessel was used mainly on the Vancouver–Bella Coola–Skeena River run, because of her greater cargo capacity and the need for freighting enormous amounts of canned salmon to Vancouver. In 1907 the *Camosun* was outfitted with a wireless telegraph, the first steamer on the coast to have one.

The *Venture* was the first Union boat that I recall. It was very grand to a little girl who had

The Comox *at dock. Note the below-deck cabins.*

only seen small gas boats and rowboats. The *Venture* had first-, second- and third-class accommodation. First class was the top deck, nice fresh air, windows instead of portholes, and you could stroll on deck in nice weather. It wasn't too nice in storms, though; the roll was worse, and a person could get wet going to and from the dining room. Second class was the main deck; each stateroom had an upper and lower bunk and a short settee. There was one chair, a let-down basin, and running water—both hot and cold—which was a real novelty for me. When the basin was tipped up, the water emptied out and the basin snapped into the wall, revealing a mirror. Below the mirror was a cupboard containing a commode. There was room to hang about two items of clothing in a little niche, and the suitcases were stashed under the bed. When the occupants were off to breakfast, the steward cleaned the room and made everything shipshape. Each stateroom had a porthole, which had to be firmly closed during bad weather. Third class was pretty awful. There were iron posts, to which iron beds with flat springs were attached two or three high, depending on the head room. There was barely room to get between these tiers of beds. No mattresses – the men (and women) had their own bedding or did without. The occupants consisted mainly of Indian families, Chinese men, and down-and-out loggers heading back to camp after

fog horn; that is, they would blast the horn, then listen for the echo and be able to tell how far they were from shore. I loved travelling by the Union Steamships; it was a real adventure. The stewards treated us like royalty, and we had a wonderful time. The fares were reasonable too, though money was very scarce in those days, and often we didn't get to the "big city" when we wanted to.

One trip to Vancouver was very exciting for me. It was the trip I took with Uncle Ben Willett,

The Venture *landing at Simoom Sound.*

a "big blow" in Vancouver. The smell wasn't too rosy at the best of times, but just imagine what it would be like when it was crowded and stormy at the same time and two or three occupants got seasick!

One time Aunt Lottie and her five children were travelling on the *Venture*, going back upcoast to their home. Apparently the kitchen had been fumigated while the boat was in Vancouver, because the cockroaches had moved up a deck to the cabins. She said the place was crawling with them, and it was so bad they were even coming out in the daylight.

The *Chelohsin* was another Union boat that served our neck of the woods. All the boats made their runs, rough weather or not, clear or foggy, year after year, with surprisingly few incidents or accidents. In the early days the navigation was mainly by sight and compass. When it was foggy, some men were very good at sounding with the

after he had cut his leg quite badly and it just didn't seem to be healing well. Uncle Ben and Aunt Ada didn't have any children and were almost like a mother and father to me. When we got on the boat at Bond Sound, Uncle Ben was paying his fare when the purser asked him how old I was. "Oh, she's five or five and a half," said Uncle Ben. I spoke right up and said to the purser, "I'm six years old!" The purser, of course, had no choice but to charge half fare for me. I didn't hear the last of that one for years to come; I think it cost my uncle five dollars.

The dining was the best part of any trip. The head steward came around, tapping his little xylophone and calling "First call for breakfast," or whatever meal it was. In a half hour or more, he would come around again, first the music, then "second call." The meals were very good, with at least two choices for the main course. There was soup, salad, fish, main course and dessert, followed by a finger bowl with a warm towel. Cloth napkins were used, and sterling silver cutlery and serving dishes. The table stewards did everything in their power to make your meal a memorable experience. Midnight lunch was also served. Any suitable leftovers were laid out, plus bread, cheese, cold cuts, cake, cookies, pie, tea and coffee.

When we travelled to Vancouver as a family, one stateroom was as much as our budget would allow. Shirley and Barbara slept in the upper bunk, Mother and I in the lower bunk and Ted on the settee. That left Dad to fend for himself. Actually, that was the part of the trip he liked best. He would look around to see who was on the boat and then arrange for an all-night solo game. The next morning at breakfast, he would tell us all about the game, how much he won (he was a good player and usually pretty lucky) and all the interesting things that had happened. After breakfast, Dad went to bed, and we stayed clear of the stateroom until noon.

Captain Bob Wilson of the *Chelohsin* was the perfect man for the logging camp run. He was a quiet, competent man and very respected. But by the late thirties, a few people were finding out that a round trip on the northern run was a real nice experience, although the ship's crew, including the captain, were really not geared for the tourist trade. Now, our shy but courageous captain had many accomplishments, but handling tourists — especially female ones — was not one of them. On one memorable trip, three women gave Captain Wilson more grey hairs than he really needed. It was a three-generation group: mother, daughter, and granddaughter. The mother inspected the whole ship and lorded it over others during meals as if she owned the vessel, while the granddaughter followed the captain around and generally made a nuisance of herself. The daughter took a different view of the situation — here was a man who couldn't get away, and it was a wonderful time for a shipboard romance! All day Captain Wilson had to put up with these three, and by late evening he was getting pretty frazzled, so one night he decided to go to midnight lunch early and try to avoid them. He was out of luck. As soon as he got to the dining room, the mother came over and started gushing about the trip, the scenery, the food, the service and everything else

she could think of. In his hurry to get back to the safety of the bridge, the captain put raspberry jam in his tea, instead of on his toast. "Oh Captain, you put the jam in your tea!" she twittered. He replied, "That's the way I like it," and stalked off, very red-faced and muttering to himself.

With the advance of flying and telephones after the Second World War, the steamship service declined. Soon most people were flying to Vancouver and other places, appreciating the speed and comfort. But it is nice to remember those former times, the friendly service, leisurely dining and visiting with good friends.

In 1907 the Moores had their camp towed up to Drury Inlet from Jervis Inlet by the *Coutli*. She was a steam tug owned by the Union Steamship Company. The children were allowed the run of the ship and really enjoyed the trip. On the way they went aground in Chatham Channel and had to wait for several hours to get floating again. During the wait the men from the camp captured two baby eagles and gave them to Ada, Everett and Dad. It was great fun, and the birds became very tame, following the children around on the beach, waiting for rocks to be turned over so they could eat the eels. Dad said the young eagles ate so many eels that they kept wriggling back out of their beaks. The poor things died in a short time, probably from being overfed.

The Cassiar, *about 1903.*

Minstrel Island

IN 1905 OSCAR SODERMAN handlogged on Minstrel Island, opposite Gilford Island on Knight Inlet. He built a shack where the settlement now exists. Many areas on the island were suitable for handlogging, as the island sloped steeply and the logs could be skidded easily into the water. The bay that shelters the buildings and wharf is also a protected booming ground.

Over the years many different logging outfits logged on Minstrel Island, and many more were in the vicinity. This little settlement was the link with civilization for loggers and fishermen in the area. Once a week, after the Union Steamship Company established the northern run and made Minstrel one of the stops, loggers from the area swarmed there to pick up freight and mail. Boat day was a real occasion. In those early years, the only forms of communication were word-of-mouth

and writing. No radios, telephones or such like were in existence around there, so when boat day came along, everyone exchanged news and listened for news from Vancouver.

By 1905 Minstrel Island had one hotel, and in 1922 Neil Hood added to the complex by moving over the disused hotel from Port Harvey on Cracroft Island. With two hotels and a store, this tiny place became a real centre for the hundreds of loggers beavering away on the surrounding islands, inlets and bays. Some poor fellows arrived at Minstrel on their way to Vancouver to see the bright lights and never even got as far as the Union steamer. They would go to the beer parlour to wait for the Union boat, and by the time the whistle finally blew to signal the boat's departure they would be past caring. By the time the next boat day rolled around, they would be broke, so it was back to the hillsides again.

Roy Halliday of the Kingcome Hallidays had the store at Minstrel Island during the 1930s and sold it to Ben Reid in 1940. Roy and his wife Georgie lived ashore, but the store was on a float tied up at the side of the wharf. Roy was a man to remember: he had lost one foot to tuberculosis of the bone, but worked side by side with the best of them. He logged and even worked on the boom, where being quick on your feet is essential.

As children we were lucky to get to Minstrel Island five or six times a year, so it was a real treat when we did. My earliest memory of Minstrel is going to the store and picking out my own candy bar. I usually chose McIntosh toffee because it lasted the longest, and I would ration it out to myself to make it last even longer. It was a good bargain for five cents. When the boat came in and freight was delivered, all interested parties congregated at the store to get ice cream. The Union boat had a small freezer but the store didn't, so ice cream melted in a few hours. They usually only had one kind—strawberry, chocolate or vanilla—but the cones were stacked high, and five cents did the trick.

One trip we took to Minstrel would be hard to forget. It was wintertime, and I suppose Mom and Dad were craving a bit of excitement. Why else would they have considered going to a dance on Minstrel Island on Saturday night? Amidy (Middy) Levesque was going to pick us all up on his way, and he was late getting to our place. It must have been nearly eight o'clock by the time he arrived, and it was starting to blow. Anyway, we took off, six of us and the eight who were already on the boat. Middy had a good boat, around thirty-two feet, with a reliable gas engine. It had a small skiff pulled up at the back, but no life belts or flotation devices of any kind. As we headed into Knight Inlet, the waves got pretty bad and the boat started to pound. Mrs. Levesque got frightened and demanded that Middy turn around and take her home. That wasn't too easy to do because he didn't want to go broadside to the waves, but he made it, took her home, and in a few more minutes we were on our way again. By this time it wasn't only Mrs. Levesque who was frightened because it was pitch dark and very rough. There were about eight of us, down below where the engine was, sitting around in a half-circle, breathing engine and bilge water fumes. I wasn't too popular after I lost my supper all over Albert Laviolette. We

Oscar Soderman's float camp in Knight Inlet.

finally made it to Minstrel and were very thankful that nothing worse had happened.

The dances at Minstrel were fun-filled events. They would start about nine in the evening with a few people plus children, then just before eleven-thirty most of the children were put to bed, the beer parlour would close and the dance would liven up. In the morning we children would get up and go looking for beer bottles to sell, and Mom and Dad would just be going to bed for a couple of hours sleep. Then off we would go in the boat for home. Mom loved dancing, but her old foot injury would give her pain for days afterward.

Minstrel Island could boast of having the shortest road in the province. From the end of the wharf to the hotel was probably sixty to seventy feet, and the wharf was perhaps a hundred yards. On boat day, the little truck owned by the hotel was kept busy backing down the road and wharf loaded with "empties," then going forward to the hotel loaded with "fulls." The truck never turned around because the wharf was too small and narrow.

Minstrel Island has had its share of characters over the years too. Old Tom Hintula lived on his boat at Minstrel for years. At first he fished a bit to keep body and soul together, but as the years went by he fished less and bootlegged more. Boat days were good for him because he sold the odd bottle and made a little money. He wasn't above drinking up some of his profits either. Tom was a good storyteller, and I used to sit fascinated, listening to his tall tales. Albert London used to visit Minstrel often in those days. He was a logger and worked at many of the camps in the area. Everyone called him "Long Albert," I suppose because he was tall and slim. He liked his beer and would head up to the hotel as soon as the camp boat landed at the dock. "Big Henry" Meittenin was another local character. Footloose, hard-working, he was loyal to his boss but seldom stayed at one camp very long. The lure of the "bright lights" of Vancouver was strong, especially for the single men. They would spend all their money in the city, then hire out again to a camp in the same general area.

We sometimes visited the Macdonalds when we were at Minstrel. Jack, Dot and family lived there on a float house, and Jack repaired boats and built rowboats. Dot was a Halliday, so isolation held no terrors for her. They later moved to Lagoon Cove — still close to Minstrel — and when she became a widow Dot moved to Victoria to live. She loved to talk of the days upcoast, especially of spring salmon fishing at dusk when they were in Lagoon Cove.

While Minstrel Island was our link with civilization, sometimes civilization came to us in the form of the travelling salesman. These men usually travelled in nice boats, perhaps thirty or more feet in length, with bunks and a galley. They were always invited to eat at the camp but could provide their own meals if necessary. They would stop in at the camps about once a year, or more often if business warranted it.

One man came to our camp two or three times to sell vegetables. He came in the fall, in an old converted gillnetter loaded down with potatoes, carrots, turnips, onions and boxes of different kinds of apples. We sure enjoyed the fresh apples and the variety of apple desserts after his visits too. He also bought beer bottles for ten cents a dozen. The bottles were put into empty potato sacks, and it didn't seem to bother him if he broke one or two, although we were appalled.

Jack Scothorn was a salesman we were always excited to see — a poker game was almost a certainty that evening! He sold insurance of all kinds, including our essential fire insurance. One time Dad bought a life insurance policy from him. It matured after twenty years, and by that time we were at Gibsons Landing, but it was exciting talking over what was to be done with the money. It was only five thousand dollars, but in those days that was a lot. Strangely enough, the money was used to get back into logging after Dad sold out at Gibsons.

Occasionally a forestry boat would come along, carrying a timber cruiser to look at a claim. The names of these boats always started with the word *Western*. There was the *Western Cedar*, *Western Spruce* and several others.

Minstrel Island has changed over the years. The hotel is gone, the dance hall is fallen down, and only the store remains in operation. Since the passing of the small independent logging outfits there is little reason for places like that to grow.

My sisters Shirley and Barbara Kimball with John, Betsie and Frances Macdonald at Minstrel Island.

Oh, the Fishing!

YOU MUST HAVE HEARD MANY STORIES about fishing, but have you ever heard of someone catching a salmon without going fishing, or without even trying to fish? In fact, this salmon was caught while the persons involved were sleeping. No, they weren't using a gillnet, and no, it wasn't a seine net either. And they didn't have a set line. This happened in Quatsi Bay in the 1920s. Uncle Frank and two other men were sleeping in the bunkhouse on a September morning, when they were awakened by a persistent flap, flap, flapping. They went out to investigate and found that a good sized coho salmon had jumped into the rowboat that had been pulled up onto the float. Great-Grandma Anderson was sure surprised when the men presented it to her at breakfast.

The salmon runs were a sight to behold in those days. Even I can remember, as a child, seeing salmon fill a creek from one side to the other, so you couldn't see bottom. You couldn't see the end of them, looking upstream or down. And I'm not just talking about the lowly humpy. The coho, spring and sockeye salmon were just as thick in the early 1900s.

In 1901 there was a record-breaking sockeye run, with 1.2 million cases canned. The fishing was so good that at times the canneries couldn't keep up, and many fish were dumped because they were too old to process. This occurred in the best fishing years, and many times the fisherman didn't get paid for his catch, or was paid for only part of it because of the overflow.

The first cannery on the British Columbia coast opened in 1870, and by the end of the century there were almost too many to count. Every river was supplying fish that were sent to England and

1928: Earl Broyles, Aunt Flo Broyles, Grandma Moore, Aunt Agnes Murray, Mrs. Edwards, Uncle Ed, Aunt Ada Willett, Aunt Ethel, Uncle Everett and Grampa Charlie Moore.

S.S. Chelohsin, *a frequent visitor on the logging camp run.*

the Continent. Of course, it couldn't last; probably the amazing thing is that it lasted as long as it did. Amazing too is the fact that fishing is still a major industry in British Columbia today.

There was a big run of salmon every year in most of the rivers and creeks. The handloggers didn't do much damage in the forest, but the bigger logging outfits with horses and steam donkeys were beginning to. It was such a big country, with so much timber and so many rivers and creeks that it didn't seem possible that whole river systems could be ruined, and that people would fight over the right to fish where they chose. Now we know the damage that can be done to the ecology; unfortunately not near enough is being done to remedy it.

Fishermen and people profiting from fish soon became greedy. Canneries were built all up and down the coast. This vast bonanza, this neverending river of fish, had to be plundered. The waste was incredible, and the rape was criminal. The fisheries officers were few and far between, using slow boats to try to enforce the laws. Seine boats and gillnetters set their nets at creek and river mouths in flagrant disobedience of the laws, knowing they were in little danger of being caught. In Bond Sound, in the 1930s, the seiners ran

almost to the head of the bay, set their nets, and then slowly towed them back out past the fishing boundary signs. Then they brailed out their catch at their leisure. I watched them do this as a child and remember Uncle Ben being disgusted over it.

All you needed to catch a salmon back in the "good old days" was a hank of green fish line, a weight and a spoon. Catch More was one of the early spoons, patented in 1918. Diamond, McMahon, Wonder and countless others soon followed. Before that, people made their own, and very ingenious some of them were too.

Soon after Mother and Dad were married, a school of salmon came in close to their float, slowly swimming by on the way to the spawning creek. Mom decided she would have a try at one, so she tossed a spoon and line out as far as she could and slowly retrieved it. She could see a great black mass of fish, and every once in a while one would, for no apparent reason, jump out of the water. The jumping salmon were what had made her notice them in the first place. At the second throw a salmon bit, and the men were sure surprised to see a nice coho when they came home from work, especially when they knew there wasn't even a rowboat in camp that day.

Schools

WHEN MY FATHER, with his family, went "up north" — as we always seemed to call it — there were no schools. But a good education could be obtained by correspondence, and the family took advantage of this for a number of years. Grandma Moore was literate, but not well educated, so she wasn't much help, except to make the children "toe the line." However, Mr. Whitman — the bookkeeper at Emerson's camp, where the Moore men worked at first — got them started on the right foot. Then, in 1912, Grampa Charlie bought a house in Vancouver and Gram Moore and the children stayed there during the school year. In the summer, as soon as school was over, it was back up north, and happy to go too.

By the time I was ready to go to school, things hadn't changed much, although Simoom Sound had had a school from 1929 to 1934. The Dunseiths, with some help from other families, had to pay the teacher because there weren't enough pupils for the local school board to send one. It cost them the princely sum of $955.20 per annum. In the school year of 1933–34, Miss E. Girling taught school at Simoom Sound for seven pupils and received $1,479.00 a year. In 1935 a school opened at Echo Bay, only because I was allowed to start at the age of five. This made enough pupils so the government had to pay for a teacher. A good thing too, because I'm sure my folks wouldn't have been able to afford the cost.

This was a very exciting time for me. The school was ashore, and we all walked together, past the teacher's house, along a path fringed by salmonberry bushes and stinging nettles, across an open field, past the old mill and along a bit farther to the school. It seemed a long way to me, especially at first, but it was probably no more than five or six hundred yards. The old mill was very interesting. Even in those days it had been abandoned for about thirty years. We loved to explore around it, and play hide and seek. There were also the remains of a flume behind the school, though by then it was pretty well rotted

out. This was used to float the shake bolts to the mill.

The school was a typical one-room schoolhouse: a wood heater at the back, the teacher's desk at the front and desks in between. Two blackboards were on the wall behind the teacher, and each side wall had a couple of windows. The poor teacher was stuck with grades one through eight. Lorraine Laviolette, Myrtle and Wayne McIntyre, Leonard Rose, John and Margaret Roth, one or two Cato children, Lulu Vasseur, and the four of us made up most, if not all, of the pupils.

Even in those days the teachers varied in their abilities and attitudes. The first one at Echo Bay fell madly in love and forgot all about teaching. Barbara was having trouble with fractions, and the teacher kept her in after school for a bit more study. When four o'clock rolled around, and Barbara was still missing, Mother went to the school to find her. There was Barbara, in tears, and no sign of the teacher. Mom took Barb home, then went back to find the teacher, who had forgotten Barbara was there when her boyfriend stopped by. Mother gave her a good talking to. She was replaced by Miss Janet Lansdowne, of the Kingcome Lansdownes, and she soon had the situation under firm control.

Another little girl started school the same time as I did, and she also was only five years old. I guess her family didn't give her any instructions about raising her hand and such like, because the third day she was there she was called to the blackboard and promptly wet her pants. It was decided that she was a trifle immature and could easily wait a year before starting school.

After two years at Echo Bay, enjoying school life with other children and learning how to play hide and seek, anti-anti-I-over and mumbley-peg, we moved back to Port Elizabeth and took correspondence. For one year our family was all together, then my folks sent Shirley and Barbara to school in Vancouver, staying with Mom's mother. Ted and I took two more years of correspon-

Dot Botta, Ada Willett, Vera Moore and Peter Botta in an old rowboat. Note the bowl haircut.

dence, then my parents decided it would be much better to hire a teacher for us and have the whole family back together again. By this time Dad had acquired a one-room house previously belonging to his mother and stepfather, and it was ideal for our teacher. We also needed a schoolhouse, so Dad put a float together and built a small structure consisting of a main room, plus two small rooms with double-decker bunks.

Then the teacher came, and wonder of wonders, it was a man. His name was Mr. Hindle, and he was a very nice fellow, though getting on in years. Unfortunately, he was a bit beyond teaching anyone as it turned out, and after a couple of months he had to be let go. His replacement was Miss Rose, a middle-aged spinster, and soon we were all on the right track again. We used to take her out in the rowboat, hiking the beaches, fishing, and occasionally on Sundays we had picnics with her. I still have memories of her trying to teach us to sing. She was a Scots lady, and her favourite song was "Loch Lomond."

None of us could carry a tune, and it must have been enough to make the seagulls cry, I'm sure.

During the time of our hired teachers, we also boarded a little girl, Marie Muron, who was about my age. She stayed during the week and went home on the weekends. It was a good arrangement for her folks, because they were French-Canadian and would have found it difficult teaching Marie through correspondence.

At Minstrel Island they were having the same trouble as far as schooling was concerned. Finally the Macdonalds, Cabeens and Hallidays got together and hired a tutor, until in 1941 there were enough children to warrant a regular teacher.

Many children took correspondence in those early years. It provided a good education but didn't do anything as far as training children to play and get along with others. When our family moved to the Gibsons Landing area in 1941, we children were all painfully shy and it took some time to get over it.

Cooks

Frank Anderson, Frank Benjamin, Earl Broyles and my brother Ted, eating watermelon outside the cookhouse.

MY MOTHER'S SIDE OF THE FAMILY also went upcoast in the early days to earn a living. Mother was raised in the city, but her grandmother and grandfather Anderson worked up north starting about 1910. Great-Grampa Anderson logged and fished, and Great-Grandma Anderson cooked in logging camps. They had seven children. Most of them went to the "big city" when they grew up, but Mother's Uncle Steve and Uncle Frank both liked the outdoor life and stayed up north most of their lives. Steve stayed pretty much with fishing, and Frank, although small in stature, stuck mainly with logging, but he sure liked fishing as a sport. One time when we went trout fishing up Drury Inlet, he and I had blood running down our faces from black fly bites but were too busy catching trout to notice.

Great-Grampa Anderson fished around the coast for many years until his drinking aggravated his diabetes so badly that he lost a leg. He ended up in the Royal Oak Nursing Home in Burnaby. I remember visiting him when I was a child. His second leg had to be amputated some time before he died. I guess he lived a pretty hard life. Great-Grandma Anderson cooked for Uncle Frank, Jim Shope, Owen Waite and Carl Stamey in the 1920s. She had never gone to school and couldn't read, so she had to do all her cooking from memory. From what I hear, she did a fine job of it too. She died the year I was born.

Many of the cookhouses in those days had a rack in front to hang lunch boxes on. When the men got home from work, they put their empty boxes on the rack on their way up to the bunkhouse. The next morning the boxes and thermoses would be clean and sitting beside the lunch table waiting for the owner to make up his lunch. Another clean-up job done by the bullcook, the cook's helper. When Bernice Moore was a little girl she used to play on the lunch kit rack. One day when she was having a fine time there, some whales came up real close to the floats and "blew" right beside her. She didn't want to play on the rack for a long time after that. This happened when the camp Nate Moore was running was logging in Kingcome Inlet. The whales came every year, and Moore Bay seemed to be a favourite place for them. Once the Moores witnessed a whale being born in the bay.

A triangle and bar also hung in front of the cookhouse, and the cook gave it a merry clanging to call the men in for meals. And what meals they were! Steaks twice a week, roast beef, stew, ham, chops, turkey, chicken, soup, fish, crab, clams and anything else you might imagine. Homemade bread, pie, cake, pudding and cookies. There was a choice of at least two kinds of meat at dinner. Those men sure ate well.

There were always crows and seagulls hanging around the camp looking for scraps thrown out by the cook. Some of them got pretty tame too. There was a crow at Broyles and Moore camp that used to come to the kitchen door, and the cook would say hello to it. If the crow answered hello back, then it would be fed.

The cook I remember best was Angus Blue. He cooked at Uncle Ben's camp for a number of years, and I don't think many men found fault with his culinary efforts. He made *big* cookies—caraway, lemon, spice, oatmeal and raisin—and his bread was really good, big fat fluffy loaves—mmmm! Angus was always willing to prepare food if there was a picnic planned, or a special occasion of any sort. He wouldn't be able to go on any of these outings himself because the camp was running and he had to be there to cook for the crew, but he did like to join in the fun. Playing cards was a favourite pastime of the people upcoast—poker, solo, crib, euchre—and Angus was very enthusiastic. He didn't stay up late at night because he had to be up very early in the morning, but in the afternoon he could often be persuaded

Angus Blue in 1937, after he stopped cooking.

to have a game of solo. If there were visitors at the camp, sometimes they and Aunt Ada, Uncle Ben's wife, would be roped into helping get supper ready, because the card playing lasted too long. It was all part of the fun and all for the sake of winning or losing ten or fifteen cents. Yes, Angus was a good cook and a good friend as well. The last time I saw him he had quit cooking and was repairing a boat he had bought. His hands were a terrible sight—full of blisters from the unaccustomed rough work he was doing—but his grin was as broad as ever.

Other cooks came and went. One lasted two weeks; he ordered a case of lemon extract and then proceeded to drink it, making himself quite ineffectual as far as cooking was concerned. Another one got up real early and had breakfast all ready—including the hotcakes, which he kept warm in the oven. The men weren't too happy about that; they wanted them hot off the stove.

One cook was cranky and couldn't get along with John Minoff, the bullcook. He said John snored, which he did, and he didn't like John helping himself to leftovers from the meat house. The end came when the cook got mad at Aunt Ada for going in the cookhouse kitchen to make a snack for some unexpected company. No one wept when he was let go.

Another cook at my Uncle Ben's camp had a rather unusual experience. A trip was planned to the head of Bond Sound to collect some animal droppings, kelp and dead salmon to put in the flower boxes around the house and office. On the way home the cook was sitting on the gunwale opposite the flywheel of the *Chaleur*, my aunt's little boat. Aunt Ada and John Minoff were sitting at the stern, and the "fertilizer" was in a couple of boxes on the seat in front of the engine. They didn't notice, but the vibration of the boat gradually caused the boxes to slide. Finally one fell, and the mess slid to the engine's flywheel, which flicked it up onto the cook. There was the poor cook with pieces of offal being spattered onto his white clothes and nowhere to move to. What a mess!

Picnics

IN THE TWENTIES, a ten-hour day and a six-day working week were normal, as long as there was enough daylight. The camps were isolated, sometimes separated by several hours' travel by boat. There were no churches except for the occasional visit from a travelling one, notably the Columbia Coast Mission. Things didn't change much in the thirties either, except the eight-hour day came into being.

Sunday was a day off, but there was always plenty to do. The men washed clothes, had a bath, shaved — or didn't. The fallers had saws and axes to sharpen, or maybe a new springboard to make. There were always new chokers needed — they wore out pretty fast — and engines often required some "monkey-wrenching." The men didn't usually work hard on Sunday, but they kept busy and got ready for the coming week.

Sometimes in the late spring or summer a picnic was planned. These weren't the casual affairs that folks have now. Usually they were combined with trout fishing or berry picking, or both, and sometimes it was an overnight excursion. In our area popular places were Thompson Sound, Bond Sound or Viner Sound. Viner was best because we never encountered any bears, and in my time no logging was going on there so the fishing was good.

One picnic I remember was when I was about five years old and staying at my Aunt Ada and Uncle Ben's camp in Bond Sound for a while in the summer. This picnic was an overnight excursion. There were about eighteen of us, including my grandmother Moore. The women and children slept in a big tent — no bottom to it, of course — with one end open to the fire. We piled small branches for a mattress, covered them with blankets and that was our bed. A man slept at each end of the tent to "protect" us. After I went to bed, I could hear the wolves howling in the distance and an answering howl much closer to our campsite. Very exciting for a five-year-old! My uncle told me years later that one of the men had gone

back in the woods a little way and howled like a wolf a few times. It certainly gave the ladies something to talk about the next morning. The men kept the fire going all night — they didn't sleep much. They sang, someone played the mouth organ, and many tall tales were told over cups of coffee.

In the morning things started early. Someone stirred up the fire and hung the lard pail full of water over it for coffee. I got up and made a dash for the bush. When I got back my cousin Margaret Moore was chasing a man around the campfire. He had slipped an egg into her hip pocket, and when she bent over the fire to start cooking she suddenly had egg running down her leg.

After breakfast, Aunt Ada, Uncle Ben and I hiked up the creek and fished. Of course, no one had rods or reels; it was the norm to cut a pole, tie on some cutty-hunk line, a spinner if you had one, a hook, some bait, and you were all set. The trout would bite on anything — beef, bacon, huckleberries, or trout eyes if you ran out of everything else. I watched my aunt and uncle fish a big pool split in half by a fallen tree. Aunt Ada couldn't catch a thing. Every time Uncle Ben caught a trout, she wanted to fish on that side of the log. Every time he was willing to move, and he caught seven dandy trout, fishing on one side and then the other, laughing all the time.

We caught lots of trout on that trip, one that didn't even need a hook. After we had come back downstream to the picnic site, many of us had a swim in the deep tidal pool at the mouth of the stream. While we were swimming, one of the Roth girls caught a trout with her hands. An earlier camper had thrown a tin can into the creek, and a seven-inch trout was hiding in it with just its tail showing. She scooped it up, can and all, to the surprise of all the adults watching.

There was a lot of joking and laughing and general merrymaking when people got together in those days, but it was all good clean fun. Men just didn't use bad language in front of women

Really living it up in the late 1920s.

and children, and they were chivalrous too. They packed the women across the creek when necessary so they wouldn't get their feet wet, and helped them when the going got rough. A young fellow was packing Margaret Moore across the creek when his foot slipped, he lost his balance and they both got dunked. She was a good sport about it, though. A few years later he was her son-in-law.

After these excursions, when the fish were cleaned, the swimming finished and everyone had worked up a good appetite, we headed back to the campsite to stir up the fire and get a meal started. After all the fresh air and exercise, we were ravenous, and dug in with a will. Fresh trout, bacon, eggs, potatoes and tea from the same lard tin. Bread, pie, cake, cookies, all homemade – oh, it was so good!

Then it was time to go home. The fire was put out and all the gear rounded up and packed out to the boat. There were two rowboats, so it made the job a little easier. About two minutes after starting back to camp, all the children were lying down and probably asleep soon after. Then the singing started: "Alouette," "I'll Take You Home Again, Kathleen," "When They Cut Down the Old Pine Tree," "Red Sails in the Sunset" and many others. A wonderful end to a wonderful picnic.

The next day my aunt washed clothes, and my overalls smelled so fishy she washed them twice. When she ironed them, they still smelled, and that was when she discovered the fish eyes in the pocket.

John Minoff – Bullcook

I'M SURE YOU HAVE OFTEN HEARD IT SAID that if a camp has a good cook, the men are contented. Much the same can be said for the bullcook, except he keeps the boss happy. There are many things a bullcook does to keep things running smoothly, and a good man sees them and does them without being told.

Uncle Ben's bullcook was "Old John" Minoff. He was a short stocky man, the type that never seemed to hurry, but he still got things done. He had a very even temperament, and though he was the butt of many jokes he never showed resentment. John was from Bulgaria, and how he ended up at my uncle's camp no one knows. But he must have known a good place when he saw it, because he never left.

John always seemed to be busy at something. He washed the dishes after meals; he peeled potatoes and got other vegetables ready as well. He arose early and lit the fires — all wood in those days — in the cookhouse and wash house. The cook often thought of other odd jobs for him to do too. When the loggers had gone off to work, Old John would start on some project, often cutting wood. It took a lot of time and effort keeping perhaps six or seven fires supplied with wood, and it had to be good burning wood too, or the cook would get mad. Sawing the wood by hand, splitting it and packing it, was time-consuming and hard work. Of course there was always some repair job to do, such as fixing a hole in the water line, putting a new plank or two in the walk or sharpening his tools. Whenever a good piece of cedar showed up, John cut it to lengths and with froe and wooden mallet proceeded to make shakes. The trimmings were used for kindling. All the buildings at my uncle's camp had shake roofs, and if I remember right there were ten, not counting the outhouses.

John never learned how to swim and was always a little nervous of the water, so he was very careful whenever he was required to help with towing logs or some other similar job. If he had ever fallen in, it would have been very difficult to pull him out as he was very rotund. Once when Mother was walking over to Uncle Ben's camp from our float, she happened to slip and fell into the water. She had a bottle of home brew in each hand for Uncle Ben and John, so she had a little difficulty. John grabbed one of her arms and almost pulled it out of the socket, he was in such a panic to get her out of the water.

Being a non-swimmer didn't keep John from fishing. He had his own boat — a fourteen-foot clinker-built rowboat — and used to row standing up facing the bow. Many nice salmon were caught from that boat, and he always cleaned and scaled them before taking them in to the cook.

John never hunted — his was too gentle a spirit — but he was happy to eat anything anyone else shot. In fact, John's eating was legendary. Aunt Ada delighted in telling stories about the food he tucked away. One time at supper he had a steak with all the trimmings, followed by two pork chops. After that he had some stew and then pie for dessert. And to top it off, he had a bedtime snack of three leftover pork chops.

When the camp closed down for a winter break or for fire season, John became the watchman. This was like a holiday for him, although there were things that needed doing. After winter storms Old John had to check that everything was ship-shape. When the camp was closed down, all the blankets in the bunkhouse had to be washed, and the bunkhouse and wash house needed to be swamped out. But there was no big rush on most of these things, so John could get caught up on his reading, sleeping and listening to records on his gramophone. When Uncle Ben went to Vancouver, he did so with an easy mind knowing Old John would look after things while he was away. No man could have been more loyal — "Da Ben"'s word was law. He worked for my uncle for many years, and when Uncle Ben sold his camp and moved to Vancouver, John retired too. He bought a small farm close to Gibsons and enjoyed a well-earned rest.

Candy, Anyone?

AUNT ADA AND UNCLE BEN WILLETT had a very small house. It had one bedroom, a living room with a cot and a leather ottoman couch, and a small kitchen. The kitchen was used only for making tea or coffee, or perhaps heating soup, because they ate their meals at the cookhouse. I stayed with them often and slept on the cot in the living room, but when company came arrange-

Here I am, at Uncle Ben's camp.

ments could vary a lot. Sometimes I was required to sleep on the ottoman, and I hated it. Whoever invented something like that had to be a sadist. It was cold, it was slippery and it was uncomfortable. There was a built-in pillow at one end, so high you got a kink in your neck, then it dipped way down to the sitting section, then raised to a great hump in the middle. You had to be a contortionist to sleep on it, and that's not all. There was nowhere to tuck in the sheets and blankets so

they slipped all over too. The floor was better, so after losing blankets and sheets and slipping off myself, I curled up and slept right there. The only thing in favour of the ottoman was that it was in the same room with the company, and that part I liked.

When Esther Douglas and her son Wally came to visit us one summer, he got my cot and I had to sleep in the office with Esther. She was nice so I didn't mind that part, but I had to go to bed hours before she did. Esther was an older lady and liked her comfort, so Uncle Ben always had a fire going in the little airtight heater in the office. When the light was out and I was alone, I could see flames reflected on the wall from the heater and kept thinking the place was on fire. I would fight to stay awake because I thought the office was going to burn up, and me along with it.

The office was a fascinating place. There was a high counter on the left as you went in holding catalogues, the most prominent being the one put out by the ubiquitous hardware firm McLennan, McFeely and Prior—or Mac 'n Mac, as it was invariably called. Beyond the counter was the heater and then a blanket partition with the bed. Under the counter were shelves containing work socks, work pants and shirts, Stanfield underwear, cans of tobacco, snuff and tobacco plugs. As a commissary it wasn't much, but if anything more was needed an order was sent to Vancouver, and it arrived on the following boat. Behind the counter sat Uncle Ben's desk. It had cubbyholes on the sides and drawers too. I loved to look in everything but only when Uncle Ben was there. One day, in one of the drawers, I found a little packet of black things and asked what they were. He said they were like candies, so naturally I wanted to try them. They were tiny and tasted like licorice. One went in a hurry so I asked for another. Uncle Ben was reluctant but finally relented. (Boy, did he spoil me!) Not too long after I had cramps and diarrhea like you wouldn't believe. The little black candies were Ex-Lax!

Top row: Mrs. Edwards, Aunt Alice, Uncle Everett, Jean Halliday, Gran Moore, Uncle Earl. Below: Aunt Ada, Uncle Henry, Grampa Charlie.

Christmas

THE CHRISTMAS HOLIDAY SEASON was always a family affair. The boat day before the big event was terribly exciting. Mysterious parcels arrived, and all our special groceries: Japanese oranges, green and black olives, celery, Brussels sprouts and hard Christmas candy. If money wasn't too tight there would be Christmas crackers, cranberries, candy canes, sweet potatoes and maybe even a turkey.

One year, Mom's brother Gordon (Uncle Bunt), his wife Charlotte (Aunt Lottie) and their five children came for a few days at Christmas time. It was a wonderful time for us children, who seldom had any others to play with. We went fishing, crabbing and clam digging, played board games and cards and had all sorts of fun. Every night we went to bed exhausted but happy. Mother and Aunt Lottie had a wonderful time too. Instead of being alone, looking after their large broods of children, they were together doing

chores with one another, and their work seemed lighter because of it. The men too found the change very enjoyable. They cut wood, hunted deer and ducks and talked logging to their hearts' content.

Four days before Christmas, Dad went duck hunting because the budget didn't include turkey. He came home all smiles with ducks galore — bluebills, butterballs, whistlers and teal. The next day we all got busy plucking ducks. We had a great system: my oldest sister Shirley picked one duck, then started cleaning them while the rest of us carried on with the picking. Every once in a while we got a reject from Shirley. She made us work pretty hard getting rid of all the fuzz and pinfeathers. Picking ducks was usually our job, but once in a while Mom and Dad helped too if there were a lot of ducks to pick. Believe me, after two or three ducks, little fingers got tired and stiff, especially if the weather was cold.

A couple of days before Christmas the men

went out to find a suitable tree. They brought three home for Mom and Dad to choose from—she was hard to please. There were, however, a lot of trees to choose from.

On the day before Christmas, Mom and Aunt Lottie kept us so busy we didn't have time to get into any mischief. We helped break bread for stuffing—imagine using that wonderful home-made bread for stuffing! Mom popped some corn for us, and we strung popcorn on strings with some cranberries in between for the tree. There was some last-minute wrapping of presents too, and that was no easy task. Can you imagine trying to find a private place in a three-room house with thirteen people in it? In the evening we decorated the tree and put our presents under it. Mother always teased us by looking for all the parcels with her name on them, then shaking and squeezing them. This Christmas it was even more exciting, with all the people around watching her and trying to stop her. Then it was time for a Christmas story or two and, depending on our ages, bed. The older children were allowed to stay up a little later, as long as they were quiet, while the adults had a drink or two and finished wrapping presents, or played poker. We younger ones were put to bed in good time, but it did take a while to settle down. There were three girls at the head of the bed and two boys at the foot, so naturally the whispering went on for some time.

The sleeping arrangements were really something. Aunt Lottie and Uncle Bunt slept out in the storage shed but probably didn't mind because they got to sleep in a bit in the morning. In the house, as soon as one person woke up everybody was awake.

On Christmas morning, things got started very early. We had a rule in our house that breakfast had to be finished and the dishes all done before any presents could be opened. But if we had Christmas stockings, they were fair game, and we had fun with those. A couple of nuts, three or four hard candies, a small toy and a Japanese orange kept us busy for a while. Breakfast over, we opened presents with wild abandon—Dad by the tree acting as Santa. Our presents were simple and practical, but each one was a treasure to us. A colouring book and new crayons were received with enthusiasm, and we took pleasure in new books to read. We loved to get jigsaw puzzles too,

as they were fun for the whole family. Toy hand-guns, especially cap pistols, were also popular—being on floats took nothing away from our enthusiasm for playing cowboys 'n Indians. After all the presents were opened and we had played for a while, it was time for a light lunch—"not too much, and don't dirty too many dishes, because there will be lots more later on." Mom and Aunt Lottie then started on the dinner preparations, and the men made themselves scarce. We children worked on our puzzles and played with our new toys while the vegetables were prepared and the ducks were stuffed. Around four-thirty in the after-noon, when Mom opened the oven to check on the ducks, the aroma that filled the house was almost more than we could bear. When dinnertime finally arrived and the ducks came out of the oven, no one there would have given a thank-you for turkey. With duck gravy, mashed white potatoes, sweet potatoes, carrots, Brussels sprouts, stuffed celery and one stuffed duck for each of us, we had as good a Christmas dinner as anyone could possibly wish for.

After the dishes were done, six balloons were blown up in preparation for our game. We lined up on each side of the kitchen table and batted the balloons back and forth, not letting them touch the table or the floor. Aunt Lottie was stationed at the end closest to the stove and got most of the attention because it was great fun having a balloon land on the stove and burst. She would holler and bat it out of the way most of the time, but occasionally she missed. There was yelling and laughing going on, interspersed with loud bangs from pop-ping balloons. It was a good way to shake down our large dinner, and we children loved it. When the last balloon popped it was time to settle down and the adults' turn for fun. The chairs were put back around the table, the gas lamp was pumped up again and they prepared for a lengthy game of poker. We were allowed to watch, sitting next to someone and "bring-ing them luck," as long as we kept our mouths shut. We got real good at it because bed was the only other alternative.

When people talk of the good old days, I choose to remember times like these: families together, enjoying themselves and being thankful for all their blessings.

Earl Broyles and a friend aboard the Fujiyama.

Deep Sea Bluff

BROYLES AND MOORE LOGGING was in existence from about 1915 to 1935. Then the Moores — Dad's mother, stepfather Charlie, and Charlie's brother Ernie — moved to Vancouver, and Earl Broyles took over the camp by himself. My memory of those days is pretty hazy, but two or three things remain clear.

When the school year was over in 1935, Dad had Bill Haslam tow our little house and shack to the Broyles and Moore camp, which was tied up at Deep Sea Bluff. I don't remember anyone saying anything at the time, but Gram Moore moved to Vancouver soon after, so I guess Dad wanted to see her and let her visit with the grandchildren. Bill Haslam, who was sometimes called "The Sheik of the North," had a small tug, the *Simoom*, and made his living towing in the area. Bill was very proud of his boat and was pleased to show it off to anyone interested, especially if they were female, young and pretty. The tug had a diesel engine that was difficult to start, so a lot of the time he kept it running; fuel was much more reasonable then. The towing often seemed to be

at night, probably because of the tides, and so it was in this instance. We got up all excited the next morning to see where we were. A new adventure was ahead of us: new people to see, different places to fish and exciting places to explore.

Naturally we wanted to go swimming, but we sure weren't encouraged. Deep Sea Bluff is just like it sounds — deep — and the camp was tied against the bluffs, so we didn't get very much sun either. Gram Moore, not being a swimmer, was a little nervous of the water, and she watched us like a hawk when we were in her care. Every time we went in swimming we had to wear a ring of bobbers. These bobbers were the same kind that fishermen used on their gillnets, to float the upper edge of the nets at the surface of the water. Some were made of cedar and some were of cork, not the plastic kind you see nowadays. None of us wore life-belts in those days; the only ones I ever saw were on the Union boats. Hank Roth was working for Broyles and Moore then, and his daughter Margaret used to go swimming with us. There were other children in the family — Jack was one—but they weren't interested in swimming.

Fishing was different there too. We weren't allowed to fish deep because my parents were afraid we'd catch something we couldn't handle. There were octopus around and very large cod that were more than a match for small fry like us. But I still managed to keep Mother Cat supplied with little shiner perch. We might have liked to go after something a bit more challenging, but when you are five or six years old and surrounded by dangers most city kids never dream of, you don't question. Your life depends on doing as you are told. At least that is the way it was with my brother Ted and me.

While visiting with Gram Moore and Grampa Charlie, one incident occurred that could have been a tragedy. Ted and I were playing outside and had used some old boards to make a walk between two logs. They were set up in a rather precarious position, but we weren't worried because we were light and they seemed sturdy enough for us. When we got Gram Moore to try it out, however, it was a different story. The plank broke, and she fell into the water with me on top of her. Luckily, Grampa Charlie was close by and came to the rescue, so no harm was done except for wet clothes.

When I think back to those days of long ago, another happening emerges from the fog. A rainy day, and four children looking for something different to do; we found it too. There was a large tool shed and work room at the camp, perhaps forty by twenty feet, with a loft at one end almost half that size. A ladder nailed to the wall was the only way to get to the loft. When we discovered that place it was like going back in time thirty years. There were several trunks, the round-topped kind, full of old clothes and memorabilia. There were at least two dresses that had bustles at the back—very elegant—plus many other dresses, a collapsible top hat and other items that were in good condition, but terribly out of style. There were fancy fans, fur pieces and even old letters. These mementos of a different lifestyle in the lives of my ancestors provided many hours of enjoyment for us. We dressed up in turn-of-the-century clothes, pretended we were grown-ups living in that time and put on "airs" to our hearts' content.

Also stored in the loft was the dried fruit used by the camp cook. There were boxes of prunes, figs, apples, raisins, apricots and probably some I can't remember. After discovering this wonderful hoard, naturally our fingers couldn't resist grabbing some every time we went by. Gram Moore finally noticed that the fruit was disappearing and said it was about time she set a trap for mice. We got the hint.

The camp was tied up at the bluffs because it was close to where the men were working, not because it was an ideal location. It was fine for the summertime when the wind wasn't too strong, but it would be dangerous later on when the south-easterlies started. We only visited there a week or so, then moved on to Bond Sound where my Uncle Ben's camp was tied. Soon after, the Broyles and Moore camp moved to Rainy Point, a little better protected and much less bleak spot.

Bill Haslam—"The Sheik of the North."

Bedfellows

UNCLE BEN'S CAMP was a fair size, and when he was logging, the Union boats called in weekly. One year, as he and Aunt Ada were heading to Vancouver, a couple they knew slightly got off at the camp. These people were expecting to be met, but for some reason their pick-up was delayed. It was no problem, really, because they could stay in Ben and Ada's house, as they were on their way to town. The camp had just closed down for Christmas, but Old John, the bullcook, was there, and anyway the people were picked up the next day. The whole incident was forgotten until the camp started up again. One morning, a short time later, Aunt Ada looked over to my uncle in bed and thought she saw something moving in his eyebrow. Uncle Ben had bushy eyebrows, and she wasn't really sure, but she kept looking. Suddenly it ran from his eyebrow to his hair. A louse! Oh, the shame and indignity of it all! In no time at all the bed was stripped and everything washed, then they both had to douse their hair with kerosene. It was then that they remembered the couple who had spent the night in their bed.

Jack and Mrs. Duffy, in their later years, settled at Freshwater Bay on Swanson Island. They had their little house pulled ashore, and Mrs. Duffy was able to have a few flowers. She had a heart condition and couldn't do much; he didn't have a heart condition and didn't do much. They had two dogs which had the run of the house and were treated like children. Probably it was because she wasn't well, but when we went there for a little visit we found the place in pretty bad shape, with dog hair and dirt very noticeable. At the time we didn't think much about it, but when we got back home both Mother and Barbara had picked up a few fleas. Mom was very upset about it, and they both had baths and a change of clothes in short order. We were never allowed to go into the Duffy's house after that. We had a cat and a little dog for a while, but luckily they didn't have fleas. It was lucky for them too, as they would have been scrubbed down pretty often.

Living on floats had an added benefit in the summer. The biting insects might be real bad ashore, but for the most part they stayed away from us. On very quiet evenings a few might venture out, but usually we were far enough away from shore to escape them. One time Uncle Ben had a wasp nest in the office wall, however. He smoked them out with sulphur fumes, and Aunt Ada and I batted them as they crawled out of the hole in the wall.

When we were growing up, one of the tricks we played—mainly on one another—was putting some small, live crabs in the bed. It was usually good for a yelp or two. We finally got up nerve to do it to Miss Rose, our teacher, but she was quite unflappable. Very disappointing.

One summer morning I woke up really early to a movement under the blankets at my feet. Then something started to lick my ankle. It tickled, but I didn't mind as I realized it was Mother Cat. After a bit more licking, I took a look, and lo and behold, there were three little kittens and another one on the way! There was no more sleeping that morning, we were all so excited. I had to put Mother Cat in a box, along with her new family, but they were allowed to stay in the room. I was as proud as can be that the cat had chosen my bed to have her family in. No doubt my mother was of a different opinion.

The Big Skate

DAD HAD THREE OR FOUR HOMEMADE JIGS that we used for fishing anything except salmon or trout. Lead in the vague shape of a fish surrounded a large hook, and at the tail end was an eye to tie the fish line onto. We would scrape up the lead with a knife to make it shiny, and scrape the rust from the hook, then we would be all ready to fish. Most of the time we used bait too — a bit of raw beef or deer meat, raw clam or salt oolichan.

Everyone in the family loved seafood — cod, salmon, clams, crab, trout — it was all real good.

for food, but the thought of catching something that size was very exciting, so naturally we gave it a try. The fishermen were myself, age five, my brother Ted, age seven, and my sisters, Barbara and Shirley, eight and nine.

This special day we raced home from school, as usual, to fish. We baited up with a salted oolichan and dropped the hook down to the bottom. Right away, along came Mr. Skate, and without any hesitation bit on the hook. Then the fun started! We hollered and screamed and pulled

Behind the cookhouse, 1928. Note the planks to walk on between the floats.

But we drew the line at some things. Octopus, for one, was never very appealing, nor was dogfish or ratfish. Bullheads (sculpin) were never on the menu either, although some people ate them. Another fish that we never tried was skate. Not that we didn't have a good chance. This is how it happened.

We were tied up at Echo Bay for the school year, along with the McKays, Roths, McIntyres, Catos and other families. The houses were close to shore but the water was fairly deep, though you could see bottom when the tide was low. Most every day after school we fished from our float for shiners, cod or whatever else was around, and for several days we had seen a big skate swim by. As I said, we weren't interested in this monster

on that line, and that skate just went the other way for all it was worth. Finally we got him started up, but then, as he was coming to the surface, we realized that we didn't even have a gaff hook. I mean, who needs a gaff hook for shiners and small cod? By then Mom had come out to see what all the commotion was about. She suggested we let it go, but no way were we about to. Then Shirley grabbed a pike pole and hooked it into the skate's mouth, and the four of us hauled it up onto the float.

What an exciting day for us! All the neighbours came to see the big skate and remark on how ugly it looked. We were so proud and excited. To top it all off, our neighbours, the Catos, were delighted to get a good feed of skate fin.

Moonshine and Home-Brew

IT MIGHT BE CALLED "white lightning," "corn liquor" or "Daddy's downfall" in other places, but upcoast it was moonshine. It wasn't made on a regular basis, but occasionally some was made for the holiday season, or as an excuse for a celebration. You must remember that beer parlours were few and far between back then, and the closest government "dairy" was in Vancouver. Hard liquor could be ordered through the mail. This was pretty expensive, but not as bad as buying a bottle from a bootlegger.

My uncle Frank, along with "uncles" Jim and Owen, decided to try their hand at making a batch of "moon" in the early thirties. From all accounts it was very successful, and it didn't take them long to deplete their stock. Theirs was made from wheat, and after it was bottled didn't get to age very long, except for one gallon jug.

These three fellows were having a fine time one evening, just before supper. A jug had just been emptied, and the last one was about to be "cracked" when the putt, putt, putt of a gas boat was heard coming toward camp. The making of moonshine was illegal of course, so the sound of a visitor approaching made them pretty nervous. It could have been the police—they came around occasionally—so the fearless fellows decided to hide the jug. And what better place to hide it than in the woods? It was getting dark when "Uncle" Jim ran ashore with the moonshine, madly looking for a suitable place. Finally he selected a stump which had a convenient hole between two roots. He stuffed in the jug, covered it with a few leaves and went back to the house. As it turned out the visitor was someone they knew, and they had no reason to fear discovery, but "better safe than sorry." The next day after work, Jim went ashore to retrieve the jug of moonshine. After about an hour he came back, looking rather hang-dog and admitted he couldn't find it. The following day all three men went out looking for the missing bottle, but all the stumps looked alike, and they came up empty-handed. As far as anyone knows, the jug is still there.

Many of the old-timers made a batch of beer now and then. It was much easier to make—some hops, malt, yeast, sugar and water—and the worry of discovery was a lot less. The brew was kept by the stove until it was almost worked out, then it was bottled with a bit of extra sugar and left to age for a time. Sometimes it didn't get to the bottling stage, as some eager, thirsty logger kept sampling it. Uncle Frank was a bad one for that; no matter how green it was, or how awful it tasted, he always said, "Oh, that's the best batch yet!"

One batch of beer that my grandmother made had a very sad ending. After it was bottled it was put under the house, as there was very little room for storage. Each morning, the sun shone on it for a short time, providing enough heat to burst most of the bottles over a period of time. Imagine the sad faces when the men discovered that most of their beer was in the ocean!

We generally had root beer on hand in the summer when I was a child. We children would all get busy and wash bottles, and Mom would give us a hand brewing it up. It was a real treat for us.

Another brew that went the rounds upcoast was potato champagne. Terrible-tasting stuff, but it had a real kick. It was made from yeast, potatoes, citrus fruit, sugar and perhaps raisins, and was bottled like beer after it was almost worked out. This poor man's brew was cheap to make, and was used mainly during "tough times." I had some once and my lips went numb, so that was enough for me.

Fraser Creek

IF YOU ASK SOMEONE what Easter means to them, chances are their answer will have some religious significance. They might say, "Easter is when Christ died for me" or "Easter is important to me because that is when Christ rose from the dead." I would have a similar response today, but fifty years ago my answer would have been vastly different. "Easter is our annual trout fishing trip to Fraser Creek." That was my answer then.

There was a great build-up of excitement before the big day. We all went out in the woods and cut poles for fishing. An old logged-off area where the new growth was coming up nice and thick was the place to go. The poles would be long and slim there. Bought poles were unheard of; well, maybe not quite, but I never saw one, except in a store, until years later. Next we made sure we had the line, sinker and spinner we had saved from the last fishing trip. Then we would see if there was meat for bait. We usually didn't have salmon eggs, but a bit of beef worked fine, or deer meat. If we ran out of that we used huckleberries or trout eyes. Mother used to warn

Dot Botta at the oars.

us that perhaps Dad would be busy, but I think he was just as anxious for the first trout fishing trip of the season as we were.

We always got up early on that Sunday morning, impatient to get going, but Father would not be rushed. He would usually have a second cup of coffee and then decide to look around for a spinner or some such thing. Meanwhile Mother, with our help, would have the breakfast dishes done and the lunch all packed. Finally we would be on our way. It took half an hour or so to get there, depending on the speed of the boat and the state of the tide, but it seemed twice as long to us.

Fraser Creek, on Gilford Island, is a fast-flowing stream with good trout fishing. (At least, the fishing was good then!) The area had been logged years before, and someone had built a cabin a few hundred yards up the creek. The roof was gone, and only two sides were standing when we used to go there, but it did provide some shelter and acted as a meeting place. The anchorage was poor by the creek, so it had to be a good day with no wind when we went there.

Most times on our yearly excursion it was sunny and warm. Even if we fell in the creek, which we usually did, it wasn't too cold. But one Easter Sunday arrived bringing with it a cold drizzle, and it looked as though it would last the whole day. We went anyway. The fishing was poor, we got wet and cold, and I lost my Easter egg on the way up to the cabin. We built a fire in the shelter of the cabin, and managed to get warm and dry. Then we had a real good lunch and sat around singing and joking. But you know, looking back on that day, I still have happy memories.

We kids weren't all that good at fishing yet, but usually managed to catch one or two trout. Mom didn't get a chance to fish much, but she had a unique style. As soon as she had a bite she would pull up on the pole as fast as possible and fling the trout into the bush as far as she could! It worked pretty well for her too. Dad treated trout fishing much the same as berry picking. He would help us all up to the old

shack with the lunch and gear, then he would take off. Two or three hours later back he would come, laden with trout. On a one-to-one basis, Dad could out-fish anyone for trout. Some people even claimed he could catch a trout in a mud puddle, but that would be stretching it a bit far.

One year, a week before Easter, Uncle Everett and two of his friends decided to fish Fraser Creek. They came home with a big bunch of trout and were very happy about it. Not so Dad; he was quite mad, and we were disappointed too, because the next week the fishing was terrible. I guess because we had been going there for a few years, we felt that stream belonged to us. There are many streams and lakes in the area, but Fraser Creek was where I caught my first trout. In later years we took trips up to Claydon Bay, Huaskin Lake, Bond Sound and many other places, but I still have a soft spot in my heart for Fraser Creek.

After a long winter of eating root vegetables like turnips and carrots, our bodies seemed to crave something green. About the same time as our trout-fishing trip, we were on the lookout for goose grass and stinging nettles so we could have a good feed. The new shoots of nettles were snipped off with scissors, and it required a great number of them because they cooked down, just like spinach. The first thing we did was rinse them with boiling water, drain it off, then add boiling water and cook until tender. It only takes five or ten minutes. Nettles are quite bland when they are cooked, and a sprinkle of vinegar is good with them.

Goose grass could usually be found on points of land, or on small islands. It grew just above the high tide mark, and the ducks and geese fed on it sometimes, hence the name. When it was young and tender in the spring we liked to pick a feed. We chewed it raw too. Goose grass grows in clumps about a handspread in size, and the shoots are of a rather thick, succulent type. We boiled it like the stinging nettles, but it didn't boil down as much. Goose grass has a taste that takes a bit of getting used to—sort of salty iodine—but we lapped it up and looked for more.

Florence, Ted, Barbara and Shirley Kimball, in for a swim

Neighbours—Good and Bad

Good neighbours—the Louie McKay family of Echo Bay.

MOST OF THE TIME when houses were tied up at the same camp, it became more like one big family. We didn't eat together, except perhaps on some special occasion, but we certainly played together and shared in each other's good fortunes. There were card games, fishing and hunting trips, picnics and a great deal of visiting back and forth. At the same time, because of living so close to one another and not having other near neighbours, we learned to respect the other person's privacy.

We often had a loose "pocket" of logs, or a boom of logs tied at the camp. The loose logs would be left over from the last boom—some perhaps needing bucking—or fir logs saved for wood. One time there was a section of nice cedar tied up behind the floats so they would be out of the way, as there was another house tied up out front. The house belonged to a young couple with two children, and he was working at the camp, but at the time of this story he was home nursing a sore back. They were very poorly off—even worse than us—because of his inability to work steadily.

The men had just gone to work when one of us children saw a deer on the logs behind the house. It had come out during low tide, then the water came in again and it couldn't get back to shore except by swimming. When the poor thing saw us it became frightened, slipped and fell between the logs. It was well and truly stuck, and continued to struggle in vain. Naturally we called Mom from the house, and she decided the animal must be shot because it would die of exhaustion if left on its own. She went into the house and brought out Dad's thirty-three Winchester. Mother didn't like to shoot a large rifle or shotgun because of the kick—she used to develop a sore neck easily—but in this case, with meat almost on the table, she didn't hesitate. Her shot got the deer a little low and broke its jaw. At the same time, the kick of the gun hurt Mom's neck and shoulder and she was reluctant to shoot again. The sound of the shot brought our neighbour running out, and he fired the killing shot at the deer. He then proceeded to bleed the animal, haul it out of the water, pack it back to his place and hang it up. There was no sign of a sore back then, let me tell you!

When Dad came home from work, we told him all about it. He didn't say much, but you could tell he was rather annoyed at what had happened. The next day we were presented with a roast of venison, the only bit we saw of the whole deer. Co-operation and sharing were a necessity in the country at the time. Population was sparse, everyone knew everyone else, and people often had to rely on one another. That man's reluctance to share was remembered for years after and left a bad taste in our mouths.

Draft Dodgers

BOND SOUND is a lovely sheltered inlet, surrounded by high hills and fed by three trout-bearing streams. (I should amend that by saying that in the 1930s they contained trout.) Several logging outfits had forest claims in the area, and it was first logged at the head of the inlet with the use of horses. There were some lovely stands of cedar, tall and straight, just perfect for shakes and shingles. Around the streams there was the usual growth of devil's club, nettles, berry bushes and a few alder trees. The timber was mixed, with very little undergrowth, which made hiking in the woods a pleasure.

I must have been eight or nine years old when Uncle Ben said I could go with him to take a look at some timber he was interested in. By this time my uncle had a bad knee, so he didn't travel too fast for me. (His knee gradually got worse, and it wasn't too much longer before he sold his camp and moved to Vancouver.) We were walking up a gentle slope in heavy timber when I saw a small cabin between the trees. It was almost ready to fall down, obviously a flimsy job to begin with, but we went over and had a good look at it. The roof was made with large shakes laid over poles; the sides were made of large slabs of split cedar.

There weren't any windows and there was just the one door. The inside probably measured about six by eight feet and with the roof slanting down almost to the ground at the back, there was very little room. I couldn't understand why the cabin should be there in the first place, but Uncle Ben explained that someone that didn't want to fight in the First World War built it and hid out there while the war was on. He said that there were other little cabins in the area too, that he had found while cruising timber.

That little cabin in the woods encroaches on my memory now and then, especially when I'm in a pensive mood. It was small, with a bed, chair, stove and table; there was no room for anything else. It was dark, with no windows, and in the long nights of winter it must have been very depressing. It was surrounded by large trees; even in the summer the sun didn't penetrate. What did that long-ago man think about in his lonely little shack? Did he have any books to read to make his self-imposed isolation more bearable? Did he last out there for the duration of the war, and how did he know when it was over? I find myself in empathy; to withstand several years of stringent isolation, he certainly had the courage of his convictions.

Lagoon Cove, Minstrel Island.

Port Elizabeth

ORT ELIZABETH on Gilford Island was a wonderful spot in which to tie up a small logging camp. It was protected, with a small stream for water, and there were extensive tidal flats that warmed the water for swimming. The fishing at the entrance of the bay was very good, especially for cod. Who knows what it is like now, but then it was a little paradise. Part of the timber had been logged off years before we arrived as a family, but that first logging camp had tied up in Chop Bay, and a trail had been cut through to the head of Port Elizabeth. The early logging took cedar from the head of the bay. I believe the early camp was owned by Colonel Rawlston, and that there was logging in there before 1910. In 1931 there was an old bunkhouse still partly standing at the edge of the woods. It had the remains of three-tiered bunks in it, with no more than two feet between them. That one small building probably held sixteen or more men. The conditions must have been pretty bad.

Bruce Macdonald owned the camp that logged there in the twenties and early thirties, and Nate Moore ran it. His wife Margaret and their two daughters Vera and Bernice came up in the summers. Dad worked at the camp for a short while too. It was about this time that he met and married Mother. My aunt Florence cooked at the camp before she married Earl Broyles. Jack Macdonald (no relation to Bruce) worked and lived there with his family for two or three years before moving to Minstrel Island.

Uncle Ben's A-frame being raised in False Cove.

A few years later, when Dad logged nearby, he chose to tie up in Port Elizabeth, and we children were very happy he did. I suppose we ran pretty wild in the summers, there was so much to do and all those long days to do it in. If the tide was low we fished for crab, and oh, there were dandies in that bay! For the sport of it we chased the crab around in a rowboat, one person rowing and the other one in the bow with an oar, giving directions. We only took big males and could tell at a glance if one we saw in the water was a female or not. If they were at all soft-shelled we threw them back too. Crab salad was our favourite way of eating it, except for having it right from the shell. And yes, we did catch them with an oar; it wasn't easy, but we sure had fun doing it. The knack was to get the crab mad so he would bite the oar.

We had two or three swims a day; our bathing suits hardly ever got dry. One summer I had two swim suits — hand-me-downs — what a luxury! Occasionally we even persuaded Mom to take a dip. This usually happened on a Sunday, as she was too busy on other days. Most of the time we swam from the floats, but once in a while the beach was fun too, especially when the tide was coming in over the warm sand.

When the weather was fair we were seldom inside. Several times a week we packed a lunch and ate ashore somewhere. Sometimes we even made a fire and toasted the sandwiches. Mom always had cookies on hand and usually home-made bread. (Can you imagine that I actually enjoyed toast made from baker's bread and for a short time actually preferred it? How spoiled can you get?)

The old trail to Chop Bay was good in places, with poles across the small gullies and muddy spots and logs cleared away. In other spots the salal bushes had grown up higher and bigger than we had ever seen them. It became a challenge to us to find a way through and get to Chop Bay. I don't think we ever did, but it was sure fun trying. Of course, when we were playing around in the woods we often found new patches of berries. Many a time we filled a straw hat with berries, for lack of a pail. Mom was always happy to see us arrive home with them. We ate raw and cooked fruit, fruit shortcake, berry pies of all kinds and

different kinds of jam and jelly. And oh, it all tasted so good!

At times we went fishing for cod at the entrance of the bay. There was a small reef there, and we were pretty certain of catching something, even if it happened to be a ratfish. We never liked catching ratfish; they weren't good eating (even the crabs didn't like them) and they looked awful; but Dad always told us to keep the liver from them, because the rendered oil was excellent for cleaning guns. Mom, on the other hand, didn't like to see any of those livers because they sat in a can at the back of the stove for a few days while the oil rendered out, and it smelled pretty bad. We didn't fish for salmon much when we were young because we liked more action, and we sure got it with cod.

Poor weather didn't stop us for long either, especially in the summer. We still went swimming and played in the woods, but if it was really bad, one of our favourite pastimes was playing Monopoly. Unless the wind was blowing, we played this on the front porch because the house was so small. If that palled, we played school; Shirley, being the eldest, was the teacher. Amazing, isn't it, that playing school can be so much fun but having to go makes it a real chore.

We children always dug any clams that were needed during the summer months. The lowest tides were in the daytime, so it was easy for us to do, and we always enjoyed it. The large clam beaches along the coast had all been dug up by 1935, using Chinese and some native Indian labour following the First World War, but we knew where there were lots of clams in smaller patches. In those days most people had a potato sack full of clams hanging down between the float logs. The clams would die if left too long, but a couple of weeks was all right, and it helped to get rid of the sand. It was very handy for the cook. He or she could have a batch of chowder going in no time. Clam digging could be a real adventure in the winter, as the lowest tides occurred at night. Dad always went then, but he took some of us with him. Someone was needed to hold the flashlight and another to grab the clams as they were uncovered by the clam gun (shovel). It could get pretty cold out there and wet too, especially if all you had to wear on your feet were leaky gumboots. By the time gumboots were handed down to me they usually had quite a pattern of patches on them. Running around on barnacle-covered rocks was pretty hard on footwear. But we were always anxious to go and disappointed if we weren't chosen.

When summer was over, school restricted our activities a great deal. Mom really made us toe the line. How she ever found time to help us with correspondence I'll never know. One thing I do know, she got up before anyone else and went to bed last too. But poor weather made it easier for us to settle down to lessons, and we soon realized that when the work was done, and not before, we were free to go and play. We were required to cut kindling and always have some on hand, plus keep the wood box full of wood, both wet and dry. We also kept the water reservoir attached to the stove full of water. Pretty simple chores really, and as we got older it was peeling spuds, doing dishes, and sweeping the floor.

Most of the time the men packed a lunch kit to work, but if something needed fixing at camp, or if they were working on the boom, they might eat at home. On those days it was fun for us kids, and we enjoyed the novelty of having Dad at home, although it must have made more work for Mother. Dad had made a pair of "thongs" that slipped over his caulk boots, enabling him to come into the house without taking his boots off. Quite a few of the married men used them. No boots were allowed inside the house, but outside all the logs, walks, and boards around camp gradually got worn down from caulk boot traffic, even to the point of having to be replaced. There was always a pair or two of old caulk boots around camp. Ted and I used to wear them, pretending we were loggers. We were often cautioned about falling in the water. If we had we would have sunk right to the bottom, those boots were so heavy. We hardly ever ran around in bare feet, there were too many slivers from the wood worn down by caulk boots.

Another addition to the family arrived about the same time I did: a black short-haired female cat. The cat and I got along great because she loved fish and I loved to catch them. Most of the time there were lots of shiners around the floats, and I took it upon myself, at the age of four, to see that Mother Cat was never hungry. She was

very well behaved, and always waited until the fish was off the hook before she pounced. At first the fishing consisted of a bent pin, sewing thread and mussels from the float logs for bait. Mother always knew where I was; she could look out the window and see my rump sticking up in the air. I would be kneeling on a log looking into the water, fishing for shiners. There was a wooden live-box pushed between two logs, and I put the shiners in there when Mother Cat had had enough to eat. In the morning the box was always empty; Mother Cat was a good fisherman too. Shiners are one of the few fish that give birth to live young, so we even learned a little biology on the side.

In the winter evenings we usually sat around the kitchen table reading or playing cards. The gas lamp would be lit and hanging above, casting a shadow on the centre of the table, but around the outside the light was pretty good. It didn't take us long to progress from Old Maid and snap to bridge, solo, poker and cribbage. Playing cards is still an enjoyable pastime for our family. We also had access to library books from Vancouver and took advantage of that privilege to a great extent. Sometimes Shirley would read aloud from *Robinson Crusoe* or *Little Women* or something of the sort. At those times Mom would darn socks or do other sewing. We all learned how to darn socks under the light of the old gas lamp too, plus a bit of fancy stitchery. When I could read well enough myself I enjoyed *Black Beauty*, *Tarzan* and any adventure or western story I could get my hands on.

Of course, in the fall we did lots of catalogue reading. All those pages of toys were fascinating, and we dreamed about them over and over again. Christmas was a wonderful time for us. We didn't get much, as far as cost went, but what we got we sure appreciated. Snakes and Ladders, dominoes, a new deck of cards, a colouring book; they don't sound like much, but they represented hours of fun and enjoyment. There is an old saying, "You don't miss what you never had." We never had a radio, electric lights, running water or many things, and as children we certainly didn't miss them. But it must have been very difficult for Mother raising a family under those conditions, especially when she had been used to more modern conveniences before she was married. I'm sure the extra work she had to do affected her health in later life too.

Every year, early in the spring, the oolichan swam to the rivers to spawn. Kingcome Inlet was a favourite place to fish them, because of our friendship with the Hallidays, and Dad always tried to make the trip. Shirley went with him one year and had a wonderful time. The fish were so thick that you couldn't see the bottom of the river, and it was easy to scoop them out of the water. They are about the same size as herring, so some fishermen used herring rakes to catch them, others had small dip nets, and some even had small gillnets. Anyone making a trip for oolichan took wash tubs and barrels along and gave his neighbours lots of fish when he came home.

What to do with all those fish could be a problem too. We ate fresh oolichan till we couldn't eat any more, but with a washtub full it didn't make much of a dent. Preserving food in those days often presented a challenge. Mother used jars and put up berries, salmon, deer meat and deer stew. Many people had a smokehouse, and smoked salmon, cod, halibut, deer and oolichan. We didn't do that, but we always had a stone crock containing oolichan in brine. Mom would take out enough for a feed and give them a good rinse, then put them to soak overnight. The next morning she would change the water, and that night she dried them off, dredged them in flour, and fried them in bacon fat. We would have a feed fit for a king. Mmmm!

Fishing oolichan at the head of Knight Inlet.

This is after a hunting trip by the boys up Wakeman Sound. The best deer I ever ate!

Pit Lamping

WORKING SIX DAYS A WEEK and doing other chores on Sunday didn't leave a man much extra time. But besides the daily work, he also had to find some time to hunt for meat. There was no refrigeration, and meat brought up by the Union boat lasted only a day or two. Some camps had good, cool meat houses which helped a great deal. Our shack was used to hang deer in, and there was also a "cooler" attached to the north side of the house. In the larger camps they often had a hunter in the early days, or at least a part-time one, to provide the camp with meat and fish. In the smaller outfits it was a different story; the men provided their own. Deer were plentiful and quite tame, and in the winter months there were geese and ducks in abundance. Of course, there were salmon, cod, clams, and in places one could find oysters, crabs and abalone. But time was often a factor, and the hard-working logger, instead of using perhaps several hours hunting deer in the daytime, occasionally resorted to pit lamping.

His equipment was simple. A rowboat with muffled oars, a knife, a shotgun and a good light.

The most popular light was a carbide lamp; it strapped around the forehead and this left the hands free. All a person had to do was row quietly along the shore, occasionally shining the light to see if there were any eyes. The deer came down to the water's edge late in the evening to eat kelp, and they were fascinated by the light. With the quiet rowboat the hunter could get within fifty or sixty feet of the unsuspecting deer before shooting it. One shot from the old twelve-gauge loaded with BBs would do the trick. Then it was only a matter of a few minutes to row ashore, bleed the deer, gut it and load it into the boat. Back at the camp, the deer was hung in the shed, and the chest cavity was pushed open wide with a stick so it would cool faster. The next day the bullcook, wife or the logger himself would skin the deer and dress it. Before that, everyone knew that a deer had been shot because liver, heart and kidney would be served for breakfast.

Dad had a carbide lamp and used it many times to hunt deer at night. He did it out of necessity, however, as he would much rather have gone hunting in the daytime. The lamp was very handy for digging clams at night too. One thing about them was that they couldn't be tipped too far over or the light would go out. Carbide lights were very inexpensive to run—much cheaper than flashlights—and that was important to us. These were the same type of lamps used by miners, before more stringent safety rules were introduced.

One good thing about pit lamping was that the deer were always shot in the head. There was very little chance of injuring one and having it get away.

The Mumps and Other Assorted Illnesses

GENERALLY, IN THAT BEAUTIFUL CLEAN AIR—and because of plenty of exercise and a healthy appetite—people didn't suffer much from ills. Of course there weren't any doctors in that area either, although once or twice a year the *Columbia* came around and the doctor saw patients and pulled the odd tooth. However, if someone came back from Vancouver with a cold, it wasn't long before all the exposed persons contacted it. The body, not used to fighting germs, didn't have a buildup of antibodies in its system.

When I was six years old this sort of thing happened to me, unwittingly. As usual, I was spending some of the summer holidays with my aunt and uncle and really enjoying it, when suddenly I was shipped back home. No one told me why, except that Aunt Ada wasn't feeling well. It turned out that she was coming down with the mumps—having been exposed when she was in Vancouver—and she thought that if I kept right away I would be safe. She thought wrong. Mother kept an eye on me, and when school started I went too, as I was feeling fine. Three days later, after exposing everyone, I came down with a good case of the mumps, and it wasn't long before every child in Echo Bay had them, including my brother and sisters.

Years ago, one couple were expecting their first child. They were on in their thirties and just delighted with the coming blessed event. When the wife was about eight months pregnant, she took the weekly boat to Vancouver to see a doctor and be near a hospital when the time came. Two weeks later the husband got a letter from his wife, started to read it and passed out on the spot. Instead of having a child, his wife had had an operation, and they had removed a fifteen-pound tumour!

My dad was very careful and lucky too, I guess, because he never got hurt in the woods. There is no worse sound than those seven long whistles when someone is hurt at a logging camp. Uncle Ben wasn't as lucky as Dad. He was snipping limbs from a tree one time when the axe glanced off and cut his ankle. It wasn't a big cut, but it went right to the bone. As he was the first-aid man, among other things, someone else had to fix it up. Angus Blue, the cook, was elected. Angus wasn't too happy about it, but no one else wanted to do it, and besides, his hands were the cleanest. They decided, after pulling the edges together and bandaging it up, that two or three days resting the ankle would do the trick, so Uncle Ben settled in to doing the bookwork. Besides being the boss, first-aid man and general factotum, he also did the accounts and ordering. It was a job he never looked forward to, but now he had no excuses. Three weeks later, it was evident the ankle wasn't healing properly, so it was down to Vancouver on a Union Steamship boat to get some professional help.

That was the trip when I went to Vancouver with him. I can still remember the lights of Vancouver in the distance lighting up the whole sky; I thought they were stars. Another thing I can remember – oh, so clearly – was the smell. Going under the Lions Gate Bridge – it was brand new then – we were treated to the unmistakable stench of old and new food, oil, exhaust fumes and heaven only knows what else. For two days I could hardly eat and didn't want to take a deep breath. Even mud flats at low tide smell better than that city air, and when the tide comes in the smell is gone. It's hard to beat that cool, crisp salt air. When I think of the lovely smell of freshly cut wood, or the sweet aroma of the woods during a dry spell, I feel sorry for city dwellers.

When a boom of logs was ready to be towed away to the mill, it was usually tied up at the camp while awaiting the tug. This enabled the men to stamp the logs with the "brand" issued for that particular logging claim, and do a bit of extra

bucking if there was time. Cutting a sixteen- or twenty-foot log from the butt of a long tree added to the board-foot scale, and every little bit helped. Whenever there was a boom at the camp, we used to run around on it and have lots of fun. But it wasn't any fun for Ted the time he fell in and put his elbow out of joint. He couldn't get out of the water, so we ran to get Dad. Poor Ted was soaked, and he could hardly talk because of the pain. Dad stripped Ted's shirt off, grabbed his arm and pulled. The joint came together again with an awful noise, and Ted fainted. His arm was numb for months after; Mom and Dad used to rub it with oil in the evenings.

We seldom locked our doors then unless we were going to be away for some time. Around the time of Uncle Ben's accident I was playing with the front door key, and the next time my folks wanted to use it no one could find it. That's how

In 1939 the Columbia *took some coast children to Vancouver to see the king and queen. My sisters Shirley and Barbara went on the voyage.*

Mother found out I was getting deaf. She said, "Florence, where did you put the front door key?" but I didn't hear her. So Mom and Dad tried talking to me when my head was turned, and most of the time I paid no attention. They were worried no doubt, and the next time the *Columbia* stopped in, they had the doctor check me out. Sure enough, I could hardly hear his pocket watch ticking. The doctor said my tonsils and adenoids were greatly enlarged and should be removed. Of course Mother couldn't take me to Vancouver because the other children had to be looked after, and Dad had to work, so that was why I went down with Uncle Ben. Aunt Ada was in Vancouver already, so it worked out just fine. Uncle Ben's ankle was properly stitched, and I had my tonsils out, but for years afterwards I kept getting asked, "Where did you put the front door key?"

Indians

WE DIDN'T SEE VERY MANY INDIANS upcoast, unless we went to Alert Bay, Minstrel Island or perhaps one of the canneries. There were many Natives in the area, but we didn't visit although Dad knew a few of them.

One time when I was quite young, a flotilla of canoes paddled by our camp on their way to Alert Bay. There must have been some special "do" because many of the Indians owned gas boats by that time. One of the canoes was very large—a war canoe, I guess—holding twenty or more people, and it had a figurehead on the bow. There were at least fifteen smaller canoes, besides.

The Indian village of Mamalilaculla was on Village Island, quite close to where we lived. There were two old Native villages on Gilford Island at Retreat Pass, but they were mostly deserted. There was a summer village at White Beach Pass too, but it was seldom used. Of course, there were thriving villages at Alert Bay, Kingcome Inlet, Wakeman Sound and several other places. All the Indian villages had something in common: good protection from storms; good fishing in the area; lots of deer, berries and cedar trees; and a lovely white beach fronting the houses.

This white beach was the result of clam shells. Clams were one of the staples of the Indian diet, and the empty shells were thrown onto the beach. Over the years the accumulation of clam shells made a very nice white beach.

One morning after a storm, we were surprised to see an Indian dugout floating close to the camp. We rescued it, and for about a month we children had fun paddling around in it. Then one day an Indian came along and claimed it. He had been on his way home in his gas boat with the canoe trailing along behind, when the tow-rope broke. He didn't notice the canoe was missing until he got home to his village.

Visits from Indians were very unusual, so one day in the summertime, when just Mom and us children were home, we were surprised when an old Indian came paddling into camp. He had a boom chain in the canoe and he tried to talk to Mom about it, but his English was so poor none of us could understand what he was trying to say. Mother was kind of nervous of him, so she decided that if she gave him something to eat everything would be fine. Well, she made him a big sandwich, and he wolfed it down in a hurry, and then said, "me pie, me pie." So Mom went into the house and got a big jam tart she had made and gave half of it to him. After eating it, he said again, "me pie, me pie," so she gave him the other half. It wasn't until the pie was gone and the Indian was gone too, that we all realized he wanted to pay for the sandwich when he said "me pie!" When Dad came home that night, his rather unkind remark was, "He was probably trying to sell us our own boom chain."

Picking Berries

OUR AREA OF THE COAST had an abundance of berries, the most prolific being salal, but there were many other varieties that we used. Red huckleberry was common, although the blue ones were hard to find. Lots of salmonberries and thimbleberries were around, but they weren't very high on our list. Shewell Island was the only place we knew of that had blackberries. It was an old abandoned pre-emption, and probably someone had planted them. Johnny Ray and his sister Georgie had lived there as children; we used to go there occasionally.

Our favourite berries by far were blackcaps. They are smaller than thimbleberries, but much the same shape and very dark purple when ripe. And oh, the pies we had from them! In some places we found brambleberries and wild straw-berries, but those you could pick all day and maybe get a small dish full. Actually, the best pie is a mixture of these berries, and heavy on the blackcaps. It makes my mouth water just thinking about it as I write this!

We started picking berries very young. My first recollection was one evening when the whole family rowed ashore to pick, as the berries were ripening fast, and Mom wanted to preserve some. I picked for a few minutes, then found a nice mossy spot, laid down and promptly went to sleep.

Blackcaps could be found in old logged-off areas. In the right conditions of sunlight and water the bushes would grow quite large and spread themselves over old stumps and logs. We soon found good places to pick, and filled our

John Macdonald, grandson of the old Hallidays, on his first birthday in 1932. Note the wooden boxes and handy woodpile, and the washtub hanging by the back door.

Bea (Halliday) Gark.

faces and pails regularly. Most of the time we used tin lard pails—three pound or five pound—for picking into. They were a nice size, and had handles on them already. Dad was the one, though. When we went berry picking poor Mother was stuck with us and Dad took off with his lard pail. In an hour or so, back he would come with a full pail and a big grin on his face, and tell us that we didn't know where to look. Mind you, we picked plenty too, but he always managed to outdo us. All winter we enjoyed pies, puddings, jam and jelly from the wild berries. We really didn't care for bought jam and jelly, as it didn't have enough flavour, and I feel the same way today.

Where the berries were, so were the flies. In the daytime it wasn't too bad, but in the evening berry picking could be a torture. We always hoped for a little breeze to keep most of the flies away. The mosquitoes were the most troublesome, but in damp weather the no-see-ums came out in droves. Horseflies were bad at the head of the inlets, where it was damp and warm in the

summer, but at least they just took a chunk from a person and didn't cause itching. Thank goodness we didn't have many black flies around where we lived. But we did encounter them on trout fishing trips, and it seemed that the better the fishing, the worse the flies.

We didn't see many Indians when out picking berries. They fished in the summertime and the nearby village of Mamalilaculla was nearly deserted. One day, however, several Indian women with small children came ashore close to our camp and proceeded to pick salal berries. There was a beautiful big patch, and they stayed all day. In the evening a boat came along and picked them up. They must have picked close to one hundred pounds of berries, and it certainly put us to shame. And besides the berries picked, they had picked bags of stems with berries on them to pick off on the way home. When salal berries are nice and ripe there are from five to ten berries on a stem.

The Indians used berries in several ways, other than the obvious: salal berry juice was used to dye strips of cedar bark, to fancy up their woven baskets; berries were dried in the sun for winter use; soapberries were pressed into skunk cabbage leaves and put to dry in the sun. They were then stored in cedar baskets. When some were wanted for use, they soaked the berries in water for a while and then beat them into a froth—Indian ice cream.

Many evenings after picking berries, we would enjoy a dish of blackcaps, topped with sugar and canned milk, plus a homemade cookie or two. Can you imagine my surprise when I first discovered that a person could buy cookies in a grocery store, and that milk didn't always come in a tin?

The Cascades, in Knight Inlet.

One Shell – One Shot

PORT ELIZABETH was pretty isolated in the thirties. It took an hour or so by gas boat to get to Minstrel Island or Simoom Sound and longer to Alert Bay. Because of the isolation there was an abundance of wildlife. We often saw deer and watched raccoon many times when they came to the edge of the water to eat. They were so cute we always wanted one for a pet, but were discouraged in that by Mother. Sensibly, she explained to us that they were better off in the wild.

One Sunday, Mom, Dad, Ted and I went for a row. This was during the time when my sisters were in Vancouver, going to school. It had been a wet, miserable week, and it sure felt good getting out and away from the house for a while. Dad picked a bay we hadn't been in before, and we went ashore to explore. After walking about halfway around the bay, on the beach we saw

something different in a pile of old limbs lying on the rocks. It was a young deer, certainly not more than two days old. At first we thought it was dead, but it was staring at us with soulful eyes, so then we thought it was hurt. Dad picked it up and it was just limp, so he sat down with it on his lap and let us all pet it. Naturally we wanted to keep it, but of course we couldn't. Then we were worried that perhaps the mother deer was dead or something, but Dad said she had probably hidden the fawn there on purpose. It turned out that my father was right, because as soon as we got back into the rowboat the fawn ran up the beach and into the woods. We were sure surprised it was that strong, because it had acted so weak before, and it was so tiny. On the way home Dad told us of some people he knew who had kept a fawn for several months. It became very tame, and when they finally let it go it didn't want to leave. He said that it was probably shot that fall because it wasn't afraid of people, and that was very unfair. Dad enjoyed hunting, but shooting a tame deer sure wouldn't be sporting.

There were a few harbour seal around, always looking fat and sleek. We weren't very fond of them because they ate salmon and cod, and if a seal was fishing when we were, chances were we would be skunked. In those days there was a five-dollar bounty on seal, and Dad shot the odd one. It was very difficult, because usually the seal was in the water, and if the water was deep the seal would be lost, because they almost always sink when they are shot. If Dad was lucky enough to shoot one, he would pickle the nose in brine so it would keep until it was sent in for the bounty. My father was very upset on one occasion when our dog chewed the nose from a seal that Dad had hauled up onto our float. No bounty on that one!

One winter there was a lot of excitement around our place. It started with Mother smelling rotten fish all the time, and then we kept hearing strange noises. Finally one day, when I was fishing between the floats, I saw it—a big black animal underneath the house. Naturally, we had no idea what it was, but Ted and I knew it was much larger than a mink. At last it came up to feed when Dad was home, and he said that it was an otter and a big one at that. Well, Dad didn't have a trapping licence at the time, but he knew someone who did, so he decided to shoot Mr. Otter the first chance he got. Mother was all for it too, because the fishy smell was certainly not getting any better. So when Sunday rolled around Dad decided to lay in wait. Sooner or later the otter was going to come to his "dining room" to eat, but there were problems. It was pretty dark under the house, so it was decided that Dad would hold the flashlight and shine it in the animal's eyes while Ted shot it. The next problem was that we only had one shell for the twenty-two rifle and that was the gun to use because the fur wouldn't be spoiled, as it certainly would be with a larger gun. Anyway, the otter finally came up to its eating place with a nice crab to chew on, and Ted shot it right between the eyes. The next problem was getting it out from under the house. My brother Ted was elected to crawl in there because he was the smallest, and I certainly didn't envy him. The animal hadn't moved, but what if it was still alive? Ted was pretty reluctant, but after some persuasion he went in and dragged the otter out, first cleaning all the bits and pieces of old crab and fish from the logs. Dad then skinned the animal and put the hide on a stretcher that he made. He finally sold it to his trapping friend for twenty-five dollars, and everyone was happy, except Mr. Otter. I can still remember how brave I thought my brother was, crawling in there after the animal, not knowing for sure if it was dead or not.

Jimmie Moffat on Uncle Ben's old steam donkey.

Nightshirts in the Wind

IN TYING UP THE CAMP and getting settled into a new spot, the men occasionally made a slight miscalculation. One time the camp was tied up about fifteen minutes run from where the men were working, and they decided to move it closer. So one Sunday we were disconnected from the shore and towed to another spot, unfortunately leaving our cat behind. We were all pretty upset about it, because Mother Cat was one of the family. Several times we rowed back to the old campsite, but there was no sign of the cat, so we finally had to give up. This happened in July, but by October it was quite evident the new spot didn't give enough shelter. A couple of early storms that caused waves to splash up on the floats and the boats to bang about decided the men, and soon we were back at the old stomping grounds. About three days later old Mother Cat showed up—thinner, but otherwise just fine. In fact, she was very fine, thank you; three weeks later she had another batch of kittens.

It didn't matter so much if the wind hit the camp, though it naturally would be better if it didn't, but the waves and the motion of the water could do a lot of damage. Things were usually tied up pretty tightly anyway, but if it was blowing hard an extra tire or bumper was put between the boats and the logs they were tied to.

One night Mother awoke to a shrieking gale and got up to investigate. It had been calm at bedtime, so perhaps the boats weren't as secure as they might have been. She wrapped herself in a warm kimono and ventured forth as quietly as possible, not wanting to wake anyone. When she got outside the wind was really howling, and she could see that Dad's partner, Martin Peterson, was up, as there was a dim light in the window. Then she saw the light of a flashlight and a ghostly figure by the gas boat. It was dressed all in white and was busy pulling a rowboat onto the float. Not until the figure turned around and was caught in the light shining from the window did Mom realize it was Martin, wearing a long nightshirt.

The apparition went calmly into his house, hairy legs clearly visible below the billowing garment, not realizing he was being watched from the adjoining float.

Martin had a small two-bedroom house tied up next to us, where he and his "housekeeper" lived. Mrs. Forrest was a very interesting person to us because we were discouraged from visiting her except on invitation. Mother didn't want us to be a bother; living close together like that, month after month, could sometimes cause problems. But she did make awfully good cookies, and one time we were allowed to be present when she uncovered a new batch of soap to see how it turned out. Mrs. Forrest used to visit Mom in the afternoons sometimes, and when she did we always stayed close by. In those days people rolled their own cigarettes by hand, and Mrs. Forrest was a heavy smoker. We used to love watching this procedure, because Mrs. Forrest used a flat surface and the palm of her hand to get the job done, instead of rolling it up with her fingers.

Martin was a bit of a prankster too. On Sunday mornings he would stay quiet until about nine o'clock, then start splitting wood. Dad loved to sleep in, but if he didn't get up soon after that Martin would throw a chunk of wood onto the roof, and it made such a noise no one could sleep. Martin, I'm sure, did this for the benefit of us children. We were amazed that anyone could have the nerve to do that to our father, as Dad never let us get away with any nonsense at all. But Dad never seemed to get mad at Martin. Martin was fifteen or so years older and had worked for the Moores when Dad was a boy. Martin had taught Dad and his brother Everett how to handle a gun, how to hunt and fish, and good sporting practices. These things Dad had passed on to us.

Playing poker was another passion of Martin's. He wasn't satisfied until he won a pot by bluffing, then he would grin from ear to ear. One time in a poker game, when change was scarce, Martin brought three eggs to the table and marked each with 5¢. At the end of the game Mom had one of the eggs and discovered that it was empty. Martin had poked holes in each end and sucked the egg out.

Martin Peterson.

A steam donkey in action. Note the tin roof slanting down to keep the rain off. The tied-up canvas could be lowered in extreme weather.

Mother's Big Fish

IN THE LATE THIRTIES our camp was tied up in North Pass on Crease Island. This is one of the many islands at the mouth of Knight Inlet. We were lucky, as we had some pretty close neighbours. The Thomases lived just around the corner on Crease Island, and the Mann's camp was tied up on Harbledown Island in Baronet Pass. There was also a fish-buying camp at Freshwater Bay, run by Mrs. Proctor and her son Billy. Her husband had died a few years before; he was never found when he tried to get home in a storm from Alert Bay. Mrs. Proctor carried on for many years after her husband's death, buying

fish, selling gear, gas and other supplies. She was a survivor. Years later her son married a "northern" girl, one of Hank Roth's daughters. At Proctor's camp I saw the biggest spring salmon in my life. It was 102 pounds and had been caught in a seine net.

In North Pass the water was deep with strong tide rips, and it was cold. We swam anyway, but only once or twice a day instead of three or four times. My head used to ache from diving in the water, and it took a while to warm up after a swim. Mom was cooking for two fallers at the time—real nice fellows—and one Sunday we finally persuaded them to swim with us. One of them swam around a bit and then left to get dressed, but the other man sat with his legs in the water trying to get used to the cold. Finally, when we were about finished with our swim, he slipped into the water, took two strokes, pulled himself out again, let loose a few muttered curses (he didn't have breath for more) and ran for the bunkhouse. He said he was still cold at supper time.

But we had many other things to do besides swimming. Usually, but not always, it had something to do with fishing. We liked to go to Parson Bay, fishing and picking berries. Parson Bay is on Harbledown Island, and the entrance on the north side of the bay is through White Beach Pass. There used to be a summer Indian village there, hence the clam shell beach. Naturally we went by rowboat, and we really had to watch the tides because they were murder to row against. Whenever possible Mother came with us. She enjoyed berry picking and fishing, and I'm sure it was a relief to get away from the drudgery of her work for a while.

On one occasion when Mom came with us to Parson Bay, we really had a memorable day. As five people in a rowboat were too many for fishing, Shirley, Ted and I got out to pick berries and play. It was early in the season and there weren't too many ripe berries, but we had orders to pick enough for two pies, so we kept at it. As we were picking we kept hearing noises, like the mewing of kittens. Finally, we forgot all about berries and investigated. The noises came from under some fallen trees, and Ted, being the skinniest, was picked to go in and find out what was in there. He crawled under the logs and found a rough nest containing three baby raccoons. No doubt we had made so much noise the mother had run off. Well, we spent an hour or so trying to catch those little coons but we couldn't manage without getting all scratched up. Finally we gave up, but very reluctantly, as they were so cute and we would have loved them as pets. So we went back to picking berries, and soon Mom and Barbara came in sight, rowing toward shore and no doubt ready for lunch.

We knew, as soon as we saw them, that fishing had been good. Grinning from ear to ear, they

beached the boat, and we swarmed around to see. No wonder they hadn't lifted their catch up to show it off, as was the usual thing to do—it was almost too heavy to lift. It was a beautiful spring salmon, weighing in the next day at forty-two pounds. Mom said it had taken about a half hour to land, a neat trick at any time using a handline. We were a happy bunch heading home that day, with the prospect of good eating and lots of tall tales to tell.

One day when Dad was working on the boom, he had a unique fishing experience. It was in shallow water, and while the men were taking a breather Dad saw a small halibut swim along slowly, then settle into the sand and mud. Without thinking, he grabbed his pike pole and speared it in the head as hard as he could and held it there. At least he tried to hold it, but it wasn't easy. The fish kept flapping and struggling for almost ten minutes, and Dad couldn't see it because the bottom was stirred up so bad. Finally, it settled down and Dad was able to hook it with the pike pole and get it up on a float. That halibut was about fifteen pounds and provided lots of good eating. Dad said he was glad it wasn't any heavier, and he was really surprised at how strong it was.

This isn't me—it's my sister Shirley.

Whales and Other Big Stories

THERE USED TO BE A GREAT NUMBER of whales along our coast; blue, humpback, grey and especially killer whales, or blackfish as they are often called. These huge mammals are a sight to see and hopefully are making a comeback since we stopped fishing for them. Other countries are still killing them, however, much to their shame and our distress.

When Dad was a boy in Seymour Inlet, one big blue whale hung around the camp for months. Dad too had fished from the floats when he was a youngster, and he liked to tell the story of a scare he had one day. He was on his knees fishing for shiners between a couple of logs, when suddenly all the fish disappeared. Then the water seemed to get dark, and darker, until it was black. Dad kept staring down, and he saw big barnacles moving along on the black — so slow — almost dreamlike. Finally, the water started to lighten again, and then he saw the tail of this great big whale. It was almost close enough to touch. The whale had swum underneath the floats and had come up behind, close to shore, blowing a cloud of smelly vapour. He ran into the cookhouse and told his aunt Alice, who saw it too. The whale calmly dove again, swam under the floats and was once more in open water. I don't imagine Dad fished any more that day.

Did you know that whales sleep? Well, perhaps it's only resting, but anyway, they often lie on the surface at night, with only their air vent and some of their back out of the water. I know this because we almost ran over one once. A few of our family were heading home at night on the old *Ripalong* after visiting friends. It was a real dark night — clear but no moon — and Dad was at the wheel. We had just come through Canoe Pass, between Turnour Island and Village Island, when Dad suddenly swerved the boat and let out an exclamation. We felt a tiny thump and continued on our way. Dad said, "That was a whale! I thought it was a log, but just as I got to it, it started to sink, and it spouted!" That old blue whale hung around Knight Inlet for years. It used to play around Bold Point where the best fishing was, probably because the herring were there too. One time when we were slowly trolling along, it came up and blew about twenty feet from the boat. Thank goodness the wind was blowing the other way! We didn't catch many fish when the whale was around either.

It was much the same when a pod of blackfish swam through. It took a while before the fish started biting again. The blackfish really put on a show! We used to enjoy watching them come through the pass between Berry and Crease Islands. It's a fairly narrow channel, so they were

Ted, Dad, Bill Crabbe and Grampa Bob in later years, around 1948..

close to the floats. At times there were twenty or more in a pod, and some would jump almost clear of the water, again and again. Many of the larger ones had a yellowish colour on their bellies, as well as black and white. Killer is a good name for these mammals. They can be vicious, and they attack in packs just like wolves. When we lived in Bull Harbour on Hope Island, a bunch of killer whales chased a young grey whale into the bay and kept worrying it until the poor thing was worn out. Then they went for the tongue. It was all they

loving, roly-poly mammals always brought smiles to our faces. They would cavort around the boat as if looking for a new playmate. It didn't matter how fast your boat would go, the porpoise could go faster. They loved to swim by the bow, then with a burst of speed disappear ahead. Then another one or two would take its place. They would brighten anyone's day, and they certainly made a long trip seem short and enjoyable.

We didn't see many sea lions in our area, but once in a while was often enough. They were real

Some of the men, gathered for a photo on the float. The one in the sweater is Nate Moore.

seemed to be interested in. The whole episode probably took three hours or more, and it was fascinating to watch, though sad, and we were helpless to do anything about it. The bay was all roiled up from the splashing around, and a boat would have been reduced to kindling if anyone had tried to interfere.

We never worried too much about the whales, although we didn't want to get too close to them either. But we loved the porpoises. Those fun-

fish robbers and didn't hesitate to grab a salmon from your line as you were pulling it in. I understand some fishermen still carry a shotgun at the stern of their trollers to discourage them. Seal could be a problem too, although they were more shy. Sometimes, as we were rowing along, a seal would start to follow us. A little whistle now and then would get them curious, and they would swim quite close. But we certainly didn't encourage them when we were fishing.

Mrs. Barberie and the Bear

IN SPITE OF THEIR SHORTAGE OF SPACE, Aunt Ada and Uncle Ben Willett often had visitors staying at the camp in the summer. When friends were staying it was a time of fishing, berry picking, picnics and just plain walking on the beaches. Beach walking can be a lot of fun; you never know what the tide might wash ashore, or what might come out of the woods. Maybe you will discover a good clam bed, or see some unusual wildflowers.

"Biddy" McNeill and her sister Ida visited Uncle Ben's camp some summers. Their father, Captain R.W. McNeill, was on the tugs in the early days and later became a ship's pilot on the coast. Mrs. McNeill and Uncle Ben had both come from Chaleur Bay on the east coast of Quebec. Whenever Mrs. Mac and the Willetts got together, you could expect a solo game and a lot of laughing and joking going on. Mrs. Mac was a real lady in every way but one: she swore

The Greta M. — a Powell River boat — the Columbia and the Prosperative, tied up at Echo Bay.

like a trooper. But it was the strangest thing; coming from her it really didn't sound bad at all. It was in the delivery, I suppose. At that time Uncle Ben often hired two or three university students to work at the camp in the summer. Biddy and Ida were in their teens, and had a wonderful time, enjoying the teasing, joking and light-hearted romance. I wonder where Ted McPhee, one of these students, is now? I remember him as a good-looking young fellow whom Bid was very fond of.

Esther Douglas and her son Wally visited the camp too. Poor Esther had trouble with her legs, so she couldn't get around on the beach very well, but she enjoyed herself nonetheless. "Up the river" was the card game played when they were around. Wally loved the freedom and all the different experiences — such a change from city life.

Another summer visitor — and very good friend — was Mae Barberie. She was a lovely person, cheerful, full of fun and game for anything. Her husband had also been a captain on the tugs in the early days, but he died very young. One day the three of them — my Aunt Ada, my Uncle Ben and Mae — were having a stroll on the beach, not far from camp, when a young black bear came out of the bush and started walking along the beach too. Now Mae was a city girl, rather refined and certainly modest, but when she saw that bear, survival was the only thing she thought about. With a mad dash and a quick jump she was on Uncle Ben's back, her arms wrapped around his face and neck, so he couldn't see and could hardly breathe. Then, horror of horrors, she completely lost control, and my uncle felt a warm stream running from his waist down his pant leg. Somehow they got home — in a terrible state of embarrassment — and it was days before they could talk to each other normally. As for Aunt Ada, she had a terrible time keeping a straight face every time she looked at them, and laughed about the episode for years afterwards.

These friendships were firm, and they have lasted through the generations.

Old Simoom — it must have been boat day because the man is wearing a suit!

Ed McLean

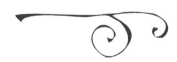

ED MCLEAN WAS SORT OF A LEGEND around our house when I was a child. He and Dad had been friends for years, but I don't remember seeing him until I was six or seven. Dad used to tell us stories about him, and that kept up our interest and made us anxious to meet him.

Ed's family moved to Beaver Cove just after the First World War. His dad was a farmer, but times were tough and he couldn't make a living on the prairies, so they moved west and he worked as a boom-man.

When Ed was in his teens he lost his right hand, the result of a gun accident. For many people this would have been a severe handicap, but with

typical determination Ed learned to use his left hand and to manipulate the hook on his right arm and managed better than most people who were fortunate enough to have the use of both hands.

It was a great occasion when Ed McLean visited us. Even Mother got excited, eagerly looking forward to talking to someone else and to the inevitable poker game coming up that evening. Mom called Ed "the kid" — he was a few months younger than she was — and they were good friends. When evening came and the adults gathered around the kitchen table we watched, all agog, to see Ed deal out the cards one-handed. With this he had no difficulty, but with some of the things he tackled it must have been a different story. For instance, in those days you didn't start a gas boat by turning a key. It was started by priming it, setting the spark and turning the flywheel by hand, a difficult task for anyone.

In 1921 Ed got a job with the federal Department of Fisheries. He had the southern patrol, an area from Simoom Sound north to Port Hardy and Bull Harbour. Some of his stories of that era are worth repeating.

Ed was a friend of William Shuttleworth, who at that time lived in a small cabin with another man on the northern coast of Vancouver Island. This other man had shown Mr. Shuttleworth his hand guns, and they had W.Q. engraved on them. From this evidence and other hints from the man, William Shuttleworth believed him to be the notorious American outlaw William Quantrill, and subsequent events seem to bear this out. A stranger with a southern accent arrived in Port Hardy one day, and shortly afterwards Mr. Shuttleworth's "partner" was found badly beaten about the head. He died shortly afterward. The stranger disappeared, and the official verdict was suicide, but there was no explanation why, as there was a poker with blood and hair on it found in the cabin.

Mr. & Mrs. Louie McKay of Echo Bay.

Mr. Shuttleworth was a good friend of Ed's, but at the same time he was not above a little hanky-panky where fishing was concerned. One time Ed had just left on patrol, and he decided to go around the opposite way for a change. Unfortunately, he caught Mr. Shuttleworth literally "up a creek" with a wet net and two salmon in the boat. "You caught me red-handed," said Mr. S. "Looks like it" said Ed. "What are you going to do?" asked Mr. S. "Well, I'll tell you," said Ed, "how about if you eat one and I eat the other? Then there won't be any evidence left!"

In later years Ed turned to logging, and by the fifties owned and operated a good-sized camp, which he called Northern Cedar.

The other Fisheries officer at that time was Art Ellis. He and Ed got to know each other fairly well over the years, but by 1928 Art had had enough. He went to Vancouver and rented a hotel room. One day he carefully laid out his waterproof coat, topped it up with newspapers and committed suicide by slitting his throat.

Many stories have been told about Tom Hyde, another coast character, but my favourite one is about the kedge anchor. A kedge anchor is used when you wish to hold a boat in a certain position; for instance, you tie the stern of a boat to the dock, let the bow drift out and then throw a kedge anchor to hold the bow out. For some reason Tom wanted to do this, so after tying the stern of the boat he went forward to throw the kedge. He "wound up" three or four times, then with a mighty heave threw the anchor. Unfortunately, he was wearing suspenders—as all the men did then—and one of the flanges of the anchor caught behind the elastic, so over went Tom, anchor and all, to the bottom. He managed to get himself unhooked and back to the surface before he ran out of breath, but it was a close call.

Most of the people up north were as honest as can be, but always there were exceptions. Ed ran into one in Allison Harbour, off Seymour Inlet. His name was Frank Bellam, and he had a little store there. One time Ed was getting some gas for his boat, and he asked Frank how much he had taken so far. Frank replied, "about fourteen gallons." "You'd better turn it off then," said Ed. "My tank only holds twelve!"

Hide the Ducks!

GAME WARDENS were very seldom seen up north; the area was just too big to police properly. The general feeling seemed to be that it was alright to take something out of season, but don't be a pig about it. We children were always made aware of it if we had a deer or ducks that were not quite legal. Mother would caution us to not say anything if we had a visitor.

The official duck hunting season usually ended in the middle of January, but Dad usually hunted ducks until sometime in February. After that they would have started to mate, so that was the end until the fall. So one day in February when we heard the engine of a strange boat, Mother panicked. We had seven ducks hanging in the shed, and she hollered to us, "Hide the ducks in the closet!" We wrapped them up in a towel and stuffed them in with our clothes, then came out as innocent as could be to meet the visitor. Although it wasn't the game warden, it was a stranger, so the ducks stayed hidden for a while anyway.

Another time when Dad went duck hunting he brought back a beautiful big swan. We were all pretty excited because it was so big, and perhaps the fact that swan were on the no-no list had something to do with it too. Usually we picked ducks in the shed or outside, but this time the swan was plucked in the house. I tried, but couldn't pull out a feather. Ted tried; same result. Shirley and Barbara took their turns too, but only managed to pull out a few feathers. Perhaps Mom thought we were getting weak or something, so she took over, but the going was terribly slow, and her fingers got sore in a hurry. It was up to Dad to pluck the swan. Before we finally went to bed Dad was using a pair of pliers because his hands were so sore. I don't know how long it took to remove the feathers, but it was hours for sure. Then, a few days later, Mother cooked it. And cooked it, and cooked it. And it was still tough. Boy, did we ever chew! After that meal Mom boiled the bird and finally managed to get it

Log chute in Bond Sound.

edible. That was the one and only swan that Dad ever shot.

From these accounts you might think that we all had a terrible disregard for nature and the laws of the land. Not so. We never took more than we could use, and believe me, we used it all up without waste. There was a doe season for deer, but Dad seldom took advantage of it; he really didn't like shooting them. And even when we were digging clams we buried the small ones again, so they would grow bigger and the birds wouldn't get them. However, I do remember when Uncle Everett shot an eagle—a beautiful bird with a seven-foot wing span—and I thought it was an awful shame to kill a lovely bird like that. I don't know if they were on the protected list then or not.

My father owned three guns: two twelve-gauge shotguns and a thirty-three-calibre Winchester rifle. The shotguns were no problem, but in later years it became difficult to buy shells for the rifle. Whenever a member of the family was in Vancouver they used to go to Harkley and Haywood, down on Cordova Street, to see if there were any shells for Dad's rifle. Of course, it was a very interesting place to browse around in, so it was no chore. They had all sorts of guns and ammunition, plus camping and fishing gear. There was also a gun repair shop, and they sold secondhand guns.

When going to Harkley and Haywood for a look around, we usually went out the back of Woodward's store, just across the street. Cordova Street was almost a different world from the rest of Vancouver. There were large warehouses, small old hotels and tiny cafes. In between were cheap rooms to rent and a great number of secondhand stores. It always used to surprise me to see old caulk boots for sale in those places. I guess a lot of timber tramps must have found themselves flat broke in the "big city."

Mother's guns were a four-ten-calibre shotgun, and a twenty-two rifle. The shotgun was a beautifully balanced little gun from Germany and had been a gift from Uncle Earl to Aunt Flo. Unfortunately, it had a short chamber, and the newer shells were too long for it unless the bolt was taken right out, so it wasn't used much in later years. The twenty-two was a Winchester pump with a hammer. Occasionally on a Sunday, Mom and Dad would get out the twenty-two, and we would all have a few shots at something, maybe a small tin can at the end of a log or the shell box itself. After the lesson one of us would be required to clean the gun, and if it was wintertime someone else had to clean one of the shotguns. But it was a chore we enjoyed, and it taught us how to look after a gun as well as shoot it. Dad passed inspection, and if the gun was clean the first time we were very proud of ourselves. Mom and Dad were both very careful to teach us never to point a gun at anyone—loaded or not—and all the other rules necessary for proper care and attention of firearms.

Beaver Cove, in the beginning.

Mrs. Levesque, Yvonne Levesque, Bernice Moore, Pearl Levesque and Margaret Roth.

The Old John

IN THE EARLY DAYS camp boats were small and slow but really quite reliable. They were from twenty to thirty feet in length, perhaps seven feet wide at most, and were built for use much more than looks. Most of the boats had fairly long cabins on them, probably to help keep out the rain, because the rainfall is heavy on the coast and bailing out boats was a chore no one enjoyed. Various types of suction pumps were used for bailing, and any boat I ever saw had a bailing bucket besides.

Among others, the engines used in the boats were Vivian, Kermath, and Easthope, one- or two-cylinder engines. They were heavy but simply made, and there wasn't too much to go wrong with them. Once they started they just kept running, though starting them was rather difficult at times. Dad used to remove the magneto from the engine of a boat we had and put it behind the stove in the house. That made it nice and dry and enabled him to start the engine more easily.

When we were young we seldom heard the roar or purr from a four- or six-cylinder engine. It was putt, putt, putt, or ker-putt, ker-putt, ker-putt, or even putt-wheeze, putt-wheeze, putt-wheeze. The latter was the sound of the *Old John*. This was the boat Uncle Earl had in later years, and "Uncle" Jim and "Uncle" Owen had before that. When we heard that sound, we knew we had special visitors coming. Even then the *Old John* was an old boat, perhaps thirty-five years. She was about twenty-five feet in length and had a long cabin with a bunk on one side, with just enough room to walk through to the engine and pilot house, which was slightly raised. The deck and through to the front was in pretty bad shape from caulk boots, and any time I saw her she needed a coat of paint. The poor old boat didn't even have her name painted on, but we liked her just the same. The *Old John* was a typical well-used work boat.

Aunt Ada's boat, the *Chaleur*, was quite different. It was a small open boat with a little Easthope engine, which sounded like tu-bit, tu-bit, tu-bit, and she used it for fishing and short outings. No caulk boots were allowed on her and she was painted regularly, so she always looked pretty nice. That type of boat was a rarity upcoast.

One summer when Aunt Alice, Uncle Everett's wife, was cooking for the fallers, Mother was able to seize some free time. Instead of resting, reading a good book, or even sleeping, Mother took fishing trips. She loved fishing, as is evident from the stories already told. Dad had bought a sixteen-foot boat with a cabin, and it was a good opportunity to indulge her passion. This little boat had a small Easthope engine, which Mother learned to run. It was the tippiest boat I have ever been in, except for a canoe. The boat was so slow that it took half an hour to get to the fishing spot Mom had in mind (we could have rowed as fast), and it was so small that she would only take two of us with her when she decided on an overnight excursion. There was barely room enough for the three of us to lie down to sleep (right on the floorboards, with blankets). The little boat had no stove, but we carried a primus, some water and a few bare essentials. Ted and I went on the first overnighter to Canoe Pass, and it was wonderful. We had Mom all to ourselves for almost two days. I don't remember if we caught any fish, but what fun we had! And every second sentence was "Don't tip the boat!"

One fishing trip in that rolly boat sticks in my memory too. It was a rather gloomy day, but Mom had some time to spare, so off we went, the four of us plus Mother. We ran out to Parson's Bay and it started to get rough, but we put the fishing lines out anyway. The fish weren't co-operating either, and as the tide came in the weather got worse. Mom said "Holy snorter, it's time we got out of here." By the time we got turned around we were a pretty scared crew, but we made it home all in one piece. That boat was so tippy we were glad when it was sold, even though it meant we were back to rowing with our trusty old "poverty sticks."

In those days, every camp had a ways built on the beach, close to high tide. This was for do-your-own boat repairs. At least once a year the camp boat had to be scraped and copper-painted. Usually this was precipitated by a persistent leak that needed fixing with a bit of caulking, or some work that needed doing to the propeller or rudder. Barnacles grew fast on wooden hulls, but fresh copper paint kept them in check for a while. An early morning high tide was needed to run the boat up on the ways so it could be repaired during daylight hours. As soon as the tide was out far enough, scraping was started on the hull, because there would be only about six hours to get the work done before the tide was in again. Most of the time any repairs and painting were done on Sunday, unless it was an emergency, and usually it was accomplished by someone at the camp. If the job was too complicated, or if the boat needed a complete re-caulking job, it was taken to Minstrel Island and Jack Macdonald would fix it.

The rowboats were well used too, and often got pretty marked up from caulk boots. Most of them had a couple of loose thin boards in the bottom that took most of the wear and could be replaced when they got too worn.

In many little coves and bays up the coast you can still see the remains of old ways on the beach. A small logging camp was probably tied up there in years past, and that is all that is left to show the spot.

Alert Bay Indian Cemetery in the late 1920s.

Alert Bay

Taking a trip to Alert Bay in the thirties was a real excursion. We didn't just drop everything and go. It took a bit of deciding on just the right time, what with tides, work and weather. Mind you, the main problem was money. Most of the time we were pretty hard up, and it was no use going to Alert Bay with empty pockets.

I was probably around five years old the first time I remember going to Alert Bay. For someone used to living on floats it was a real shock. All that walking to do! My legs were so sore that night, Mom had to rub them for me before I could get to sleep. At that time there were about six wharves where a boat could tie up, and we usually chose the second one at the south end of town. It was fairly close to Dong Chong's, where we did some grocery and dry goods shopping.

After packing the groceries back to the boat,

we set out along the road in the direction of the Indian village. Somewhere along the way there was a small cafe on the water side. It, along with many other places strung around the bay, had a very convenient outhouse built out over the water. Each high tide washed the beach clean. There were three cars on the island at that time, one of them a taxi, and just the one road running around the bay, perhaps one and a half miles long. We walked past the government wharf where the Fisheries, Forestry and police boats were tied up. Then there was the hospital wharf on one side and the hospital on the other. At one of the floats along the way they sold gas and oil. There was an old hotel along there too, just a small one, but it had a beer parlour, just like the other two, and did a roaring business. The cemetery was a very interesting place to stop, and I sure was glad to rest.

Many different totem poles were placed there to mark the graves of loved ones. There were several "coppers" too, relics of a status system the Indians used years ago.

After more walking, we finally got to the big cannery wharf. It was owned by BC Packers. This store was the largest one on the island and was very interesting to us because they carried a large line of fishing gear. There was an old totem pole by the entrance to the store, but even then it had been defaced by the jackknives of juveniles. Just before we got to the store and dock there were a few Indian houses with totems in front. Past that was the Indian village and the Boys' Industrial School, which was opened in 1894.

At this time the Alert Bay Indians buried their dead, but in years past they had put them in boxes and tied the boxes up in trees. With the body was put many of the deceased's possessions, especially the ones they valued highly. When we walked through to the Boys' School, the remains

Grave marker in the Alert Bay Indian cemetery.

of some boxes were still evident, clinging to the branches of some of the trees; one tree had a sewing machine hanging from it.

Many small islets were used as Indian graveyards. The remains were placed in crude wooden coffins, but instead of being buried, were put on boards about waist high. These tiny islands didn't have trees large enough to tie coffins to. There was one such "Burial Island" just out from Mama-lilaculla Indian Reserve. In our roamings around the area in our rowboats we saw these places, but Dad told us never to go ashore because the Indians wouldn't like it. In truth, we were a bit nervous about going ashore anyway, so it was no problem.

There are many tiny islands scattered around that area, too small to be named. One such was at the entrance to Port Elizabeth. We called it Rose Island because of the wild rose bushes surrounding it. There were other wildflowers there too: chocolate lilies, lady slippers, Indian paintbrush, monkey face and some we didn't know. Once you got past the rose bushes and into the centre of the island, it was quite clear of underbrush, but the scrub trees created a gloomy effect. There must have been twenty-five crows' nests in the trees, but no sign of crows. I had a very eerie feeling when I went in there, almost as if someone or something was watching. Perhaps this island too, was once used as a graveyard by the Indians.

Totems at Alert Bay.

The Big Move

AFTER A YEAR with a private teacher, my parents decided it was time for a change. Shirley and Barbara were in high school, and we still needed to go to a real school to see how our education was coming along. It wasn't just schooling either. We were all rather shy and not used to playing with other children. There I was, eleven years old, and hadn't ever played softball. Another consideration was the Second World War. Things were pretty serious on that score, and the outlook was very uncertain. All these things taken together convinced my parents that getting a bit closer to civilization was the thing to do.

My father took a quick trip to Gibsons Landing and assured himself that a living could be made in the trucking business. Then he looked around and found a farm for sale about a mile and a half from town. It had a nice house, no running water or electric lights, but that didn't matter because we were used to doing without them anyway. My dad sold out his share of the partnership to Uncle Everett and Perly Sherdahl. Our little house was bought by Mrs. Mann for her sons Eddie and Bud, who had suddenly grown up and needed a place of their own. And we packed up.

Dad had been friends with Jimmy Henderson for years, and when it was time to go he got Jimmy to help us. Jimmy was half Coast Indian and half white, as was his wife. A jolly man with a wide smile, he could fish with the best of them, and his new seine boat, the *Chizoka*, was his pride and joy. Dad, Jimmy and his son Butch loaded all our worldly possessions onto his boat, and we set off for Gibsons. We were off on a new adventure: life on a farm at Gibsons Landing. Little did we realize it, but we were exchanging the sweet smell of slash for the ripe odour of pig pens.

Our journey took us from Crease Island out to Blackfish Sound, through Blackney Pass to Johnstone Strait. Through Race Pass, Seymour Narrows, past Cape Mudge and into Discovery Passage. Then over to Manson Passage, passing Grief Point where Moore Brothers Logging lost a boom on

Jimmy Henderson, the longtime friend who took our family, bag and baggage, to Gibsons on his drum seiner in 1941.

the way to Vancouver during a bad storm in the early twenties. From there it was into Malaspina Strait, Georgia Strait, around Gower Point and into Gibsons Landing. It took us over eighteen hours to travel almost 240 miles.

When we started out, Barbara, Ted and Butch were down below in the engine room area, where there were a couple of bunks. The rest of us were in the pilot house, where there were double-decker bunks, a couple of chairs and standing room for several people. The kitchen table was tied up on the flying bridge, and the rest of our household furnishings were either stowed in the fish hold or sat on the back deck under a canvas tarpaulin.

Jimmy planned on leaving one day and arriving the following morning to take best advantage of the tide. All went well until we got to Seymour Narrows, when a southeast gale hit the Cape Mudge area. It was only September, but it blew

79

like a real winter gale, and that little seine boat tried to stand on end it was so rough. Barbara, Ted and I were all seasick, although Barbara and Ted had the worst of it. Every time they felt sick to their stomach, they had to climb up from below, go out on deck and hang on to the rail for dear life. After that awful session, they had to go below again to the smell and noise of the engine. The rest of the family was feeling pretty uncertain too, by the time we got out of the bad weather. Of course, all this was going on at night. It always seems worse in the dark; you never know when you are going to come crashing down on a big log

or something and put an end to the whole business. It's much easier to combat that dreadful feeling in the daytime because you can keep your eyes on the horizon. I still remember the kitchen table rolling back and forth over my head as I lay in the upper bunk of that seine boat. But we made it, and began a very different life on a farm, at first hardly being able to tell the difference between a hen and a rooster!

Goodbye to fishing for our supper and Sunday picnics in Bond Sound; hello to picking apples and plums in abandoned orchards!

Sources & Acknowledgements

Books

Rushton, Gerald. *Echoes of the Whistle: An Illustrated History of the Union Steamship Company*. Vancouver: Douglas & McIntyre, 1980.

Taylor, G.W. *Timber: History of the Forest Industry in B.C.* Vancouver: J.J. Douglas, 1975.

Interviews

Ed McLean
Bernice Lawson

Incentive and encouragement

Rosemary Owen

Help with old photographs

Gwynn Owen

Without the help and encouragement of Rosemary and Gwynn, the best next-door neighbours a person could ever wish to have, this book would never have been written.